Losing a Life

A Daughter's Memoir of Caregiving

Nancy Gerber

June 5, 2005
For Rachel,
with gratitude for your
support, Best,
Nancy

Hamilton Books
an imprint of
UNIVERSITY PRESS OF AMERICA,® INC.
Lanham • Boulder • New York • Toronto • Oxford

∞™ The paper used in this publication meets the minimum
requirements of American National Standard for Information
Sciences—Permanence of Paper for Printed Library Materials,
ANSI Z39.48—1992

For Bobby

Acknowledgements

I would like to thank family and friends who offered support during the period of my father's illness.

Permissions and Credits

Excerpt from "Do Not Go Gentle into That Good Night," by Dylan Thomas, from *The Poems of Dylan Thomas*, copyright© 1952 by Dylan Thomas. Reprinted by permission of New Directions Publishing Corporation.

The definition of caregiving on page 78 comes from an article by Ruth Ray, "A Postmodern Perspective on Feminist Gerontology," *The Gerontologist* 36 (October 1996): 674–80.

The quotations from the Book of Job are taken from *Tanakh: The Holy Scriptures* (Philadelphia: Jewish Publication Society, 1985). Quotations from the Book of Ecclesiastes are taken from *The Holy Bible*, King James Version (New York: American Bible Society, 1990).

Author's Note

Although this is a work of nonfiction, certain names have been changed for reasons of privacy. It is not intended to offer legal, psychological, or medical counsel.

Part One

THE FIRST THREE MONTHS

"First we experience, then we grieve. Then we forget,
then we remember."

—Attributed to Rainer Maria Rilke

"Language has not the power to speak what love indites: The soul
lies buried in the ink that writes."

—John Clare

Stroke.

A swimmer's motion. The mark of pen on paper. The sound of midnight. . . .

This is the story of a stroke.

When I heard the news that my father had suffered a stroke on September 18, 1995, I didn't understand what the words meant. If I
thought about the word *stroke*, which I rarely did, what came to mind
were expressions such as "a stroke of genius" or "a stroke of luck." I
had no frame of reference for stroke as illness, stroke as catastrophe. I
didn't know that stroke stops blood flow to the brain, causes paralysis,
destroys short-term memory.

The other day at the town health department, I saw a flyer that said
stroke is the number-three leading killer of American adults, and I
flinched as I recalled how little I knew about stroke in the fall of 1995.
What I know now could fill a book.

Stroke is an evil trickster. Whereas the horror of terminal cancer is clearly written on victims' faces, particularly in the final stages, stroke can hide its devastation. It strikes suddenly, seemingly without warning —a sudden blow to the cerebrum—and everyone thinks the worst is over. But that's not necessarily the case. Sometimes the damage does not make itself known for weeks, even months.

The losses caused by my father's stroke plagued him for nearly six years. By the time of his death, on June 17, 2001, he had lost his mobility, his kidney function, much of his short-term memory, most of his eyesight, and his entire left leg. During the last few days of his life, while in the throes of a fatal staphylococcus infection, he finally lost his will to live. I think the rest of us gave up long before he did.

Stroke traps its victim in a tangled web of interdependence and crisis. Suddenly, the victim is disabled, forcing the rest of the family to confront an overwhelming morass of financial and psychological responsibilities for which they are not prepared: unexpected loss of income, enforced retirement, emotional and physical dependence, foreclosure of future plans, and the stress of full-time caregiving.

My father was seventy-three when he had the stroke and was self-employed as a CPA, a certified public accountant. He did not have long-term care insurance. He had not made provisions for the sale or transfer of his accounting practice. He was imagining his retirement but had planned to keep working part-time for a few more years. He was hoping to travel with my mother. He was not preparing for stroke.

The day before the stroke, he was a gregarious, vital man—father, grandfather, husband, *paterfamilias*, breadwinner, tennis player, bridge partner, friend. The day after the stroke, he was someone else, a stranger. He was paralyzed, disabled. It was pretty obvious he would never work again, yet it's odd how the mind works: I both knew and didn't know this was the case. As with any devastating accident, it takes a long time for the cognitive brain to grasp what the heart has already intuited: From now on, everything will be radically different.

I found it difficult to accept my father's disability, the wheelchair, his sudden physical dependence. Far worse was the gradual erosion of his personality. During the months and years that followed the stroke, he became unrecognizable to those who knew and loved him.

Physically, he was altered indeed; he had aged decades overnight. His fringe of gray hair went white, his left arm and leg withered from paralysis, his face slackened, and the rest of his body grew round and soft from lack of mobility and exercise.

His humor disappeared. In place of the sociable, active man I knew as my father was a withdrawn, silent, often hostile double.

There is no language to describe such a departure. We have no prayers or rituals for the death of someone who hasn't died.

When I visit my father the day after his stroke, I am stunned. He is strapped to a flat metal slab in a cubicle of the hospital ICU. He is not in a bed, as I expected. There is someone else in the room, standing near the bed, crying softly: my mother. But I have eyes only for my father. When I last saw him, two weeks ago, his sparse circle of hair was gray. Now it is white. Even worse is the sight of his immobilized body beneath the blank sheet that covers him. He looks like the hulk of a ship. My mother leans over and whispers to me that when she saw my father, she nearly fainted.

Every few minutes a nurse comes in and checks his pulse or his blood pressure. "You know, your father is quite a charmer," she says cheerfully. "He's had all of us laughing." Oh, really? I have to admit there is something comfortingly familiar about that.

"They keep asking me who the president is," says a garbled voice I've never heard before, a voice that comes from my father. "Of course I know who the president is," says the mangled voice. My head begins to spin. "Yes, Dad," I say, my lips pulled back to form a smile. Perhaps this is what is expected of me, to keep things light, to pretend this is a joke. "Of course you know who the president is." I stumble out of the ICU into the waiting room, where I am told my father's doctors want to speak with me.

By the time the three men in white coats step off the elevator and approach me, I can no longer feel my body. My hands, for instance. Are they still attached to my arms? I feel as if I am dissolving—literally melting—and I wonder whether the doctors can see this or if I am the only one who knows. Besides, are there really three of them, or is there just one and I'm having hallucinations? Why do they look exactly alike? And what is this they are saying? *Condition very serious. First twenty-four hours after a stroke critical. Possibility of cerebral hemorrhage. Not sure of the extent of damage.*

I begin to sense their heads bobbing up and down like a chorus of puppets, and suddenly my head starts to bob up and down in unison with theirs. Suddenly I have a vision of the four of us standing there in the waiting room, our heads bobbing up and down together, and I nearly laugh out loud. "Thank you, thank you for taking such good care of him," I hear myself say while my hand shoots out to meet theirs.

Like a fleet of small boats, they turn away and enter the elevator. I stand and watch while the gray metal doors close slowly in front of them.

My father was born in 1922 in Frankfurt am Main; his name was Karl Walter Fraenkel, but everyone called him Beppo. "His father gave it to him," said my mother when I asked her about the origin of his pet name. "He's had it since childhood," his sister Ruth replied when I asked her. His cousin Lore wasn't really sure how he got it but she told me a story.

"Your father started school at the age of six. In those days, children didn't really go to kindergarten, let alone preschool. On the first day, the teacher asked him his name. She looked down her list and said, 'I see here it says Karl Walter. Is that what they call you at home?' 'No,' my father replied. 'They call me Beppo.' Because that's what they called him at home."

Beppo is the diminutive for Giuseppe, or Joseph, and also the name of a clown. There's a narrative poem titled "Beppo," written by Lord Byron in 1818, about Laura, a young Italian woman whose merchant husband, Beppo, disappears at sea and reappears many years later during the season of carnival, dressed in Turkish garb. Lord Byron's Beppo was a comic figure who liked to make people laugh: "His friends the more for his long absence prized him, / Finding he'd wherewithal to make them gay." A sense of humor was something my father and Byron's Beppo shared.

I did not know until recently that my father's nickname had originated in the nursery. I had always assumed it came from his friends, because that's what they called him. I thought it was somehow connected to his soccer days, a sport he played when he was in his twenties as a member of the New World Club in Manhattan. I could visualize him chasing the ball, his five-foot-six frame tense with determination.

When I was young I called my father Dad, but when I became a mother, I called him Beppo, as did my children, because to us, that's who he was.

As a child, I was in awe of my father. He was not like the other fathers I knew because he spoke with a slight European accent. Perceptive listeners could tell he was not "from here."

On the day of his funeral, a woman from the recreational staff of the nursing home where he spent his last year came to my mother's house afterward to pay her respects. She said to me, "There was something very charming and elegant about your father. He was different from other patients. His manners were . . . beautiful. It's hard to describe, but he had, you know, class."

My father had class? I was completely taken aback. I had never heard my father described that way. To me, he was not a European gentleman but a *schlep*, someone who preferred chinos to gabardine, comfort to style. My mother used to say that if she hadn't made him go shopping, he would still be wearing the same ugly suits he wore in the fifties.

In that regard, I'm like my father. When I say that I'd rather have a root canal than buy new clothes, I almost mean it. I would still wear the same pair of jeans I wore every day when I was in my twenties—that is, if I could fit into them.

What does that mean, I wonder, to have "class" in a society that is supposedly classless, or where theoretically everyone is middle class? What could it possibly mean in a nursing home, where illness and old age appear to level the field?

My father was born into a wealthy social circle, the German haute bourgeoisie. His father had been a successful physician in Frankfurt, his mother the heiress of money made in the Landauer department stores in Stuttgart. When my father arrived in this country in 1938, he left behind a childhood of status and privilege: skiing in the Bavarian

Alps, summer excursions to Italy. On the other hand, unlike most of
Europe's Jews, he escaped with his life.

He had the immigrant's passion for his adopted country. He changed
his name from Karl Fraenkel to Charles Frankel because it sounded
more American. He worked hard to erase the German inflection from
his voice. I had been raised to think that Democrats and Jews did not
hang American flags outside their homes, but my father carried an in-
visible one near his heart.

Once, on a family trip to Montreal, I chanced to remark that I wished
I had been born Canadian. I thought of Canada as a more peaceful, less
materialistic version of the United States, a country where many people spoke French, a thrilling prospect for a Francophile like me. I announced my admiration of Canadians while we were driving on the
Northway, an hour or so south of the Canadian border. My father
pulled the car over to the side of the road. "Take that back," he said,
"or get out of the car."

"Lighten up, Dad," I remonstrated, trying to give some levity to the
situation, but I was frightened because suddenly I wasn't sure whether
he was serious or joking. He had never said or done anything like this
before. I was nineteen, no longer a child, and maybe he really intended
to dump me in the middle of upstate New York. "Okay," I grumbled.
"I take it back. God," I muttered under my breath as the car resumed
its journey. "That's a little over the top, isn't it?"

Years later, when he was suffering from paralysis caused by his
stroke, I reminded him of those words. "Why did you say that to me?"
I asked him. "I was totally freaked out that you might abandon me in
Plattsburgh, and besides, what was the big deal about being Canadian
anyway?" I had been shocked by his vehemence and had pondered the
incident many times over the intervening twenty years, concluding that
it was evidence, at the very least, of a certain intractability in my father's personality. But although my father's long-term memory had not
been damaged by the stroke, he said he had no idea what incident and
what words I was talking about.

My father's stroke occurred in the office of one of his clients, a man
who managed the careers of several accomplished musicians. At 2:30 in
the afternoon, he crumpled in a heap and slid off his chair onto the floor.

The office staff panicked; they thought he had had a heart attack. Someone phoned EMS, Emergency Medical Services, who wanted to take my father to the nearest emergency room. The EMS people could tell he had had a stroke. His blood pressure was very high, his mouth sagged in the corner, his speech was slurred. My father refused to go and joked with them about his condition. The EMS people hesitated. They knew this was no joke, but they were not required to force my father against his will, and so they left.

The office staff was very worried. They called my mother, who was at home in New Jersey. She phoned my brother, at work a few blocks away from my father. She also called my father's doctor, a hypertension specialist at a major medical center in Manhattan, to alert him that my father was on his way.

My brother drove my father to the hospital, where his doctor ordered several tests, including a magnetic resonance imaging scan, or MRI. By now it was 5:00 P.M. My mother called to tell me that she was at the hospital and would phone me later.

The MRI showed that my father had suffered a mild stroke. But you know how it goes in hospitals: you wait, and you wait, and you wait. Finally, after waiting more than five hours, the hospital found him a bed. It was now almost 11:00 P.M. My father asked my brother to take him to the men's room, where he had a second stroke, a massive one, and collapsed on the floor. It was the last time he would ever stand on his own two feet.

What happened, we asked ourselves? Couldn't the second stroke have been prevented? Why was the doctor so nonchalant about my father's condition?

I know now that the high level of abnormal brain activity following a stroke makes people extremely vulnerable to additional strokes. Why did my father have to wait so long to be treated? Why wasn't he put on heparin, a blood thinner? Was this a case of gross negligence, of malpractice?

We thought about bringing a lawsuit against the hospital but never did. My brother was advised that it would be very difficult to find doctors to testify as expert witnesses. Too, our energies were consumed by the crisis of the present and our fears for the future.

Of the regrets I have vis-à-vis my role as dutiful daughter during my father's stroke, I do not regret my wish not to sue. What would have been the point? My father was paralyzed, and no amount of money would have changed that or restored him to health.

Of my father's many losses after his stroke, I mourned tennis first. When I was in college, I came home one summer and told him that I had met a young man whom I liked very much, and that things had gotten pretty serious between us. The first question my father asked me was, "Is he Jewish?" The second was, "Does he play tennis?"

My father was a rather comical-looking figure on the tennis court. Short and bald, his paunch bulged good-naturedly through his white Lacoste shirt. His shorts were baggy and wrinkled. On his head he wore a squashed terry cloth hat to protect his scalp from the sun. He was bowlegged and scrambled across the court like a crab. Rod Laver he wasn't. He had never lost the fierce determination of his youth, which earned him the nickname "the scrapper" from my husband. He frequently called his opponents' shots out. He was famous for these line calls; three of the four people who spoke at his funeral mentioned them. But he was also funny, friendly, and generous to his friends.

When I take my son for afternoon tennis lessons in the months following the stroke, I see a group of older men playing doubles. I stare at these grandfathers while they amiably lob balls back and forth, ribbing each other and laughing. I cannot accept that my father will never do this again. As they saunter off the court, I want to rush up to them, shake them, and scream, "You have no idea how lucky you are. No idea!"

But maybe they do know they are lucky. After all, they are about the same age as my father. As I watch them put on their jackets, I grieve for my father, lying paralyzed in a hospital bed.

Long before my father's stroke, I had been obsessed by stories about accidents.

When I was in seventh grade, my art teacher, a slender young woman with dark hair and olive skin named Miss Giardina, was killed on her way home from work when another car crushed her Volkswagen

Beetle. In tenth grade, one of my classmates, Stuart May, was hit by a car and killed while crossing the street from a local convenience store; the driver of the car was our high school music teacher. I began to think of the world as a pretty dangerous place.

I was prepared for flight. My father's exile from Germany had taught me that life was fraught with terror and uncertainty. What if my parents were murdered, and my brother and I ended up as orphans? What if a robber broke into our house while we were asleep, and I was the only one who heard? What if I drowned in the lake at sleepaway camp? What if the Nazi storm troopers showed up at our front door after school?

I once described these fears to a woman I knew, who told me that she, too, suffered from constant worry and anxiety. She said it wasn't our fault; it was in our blood, she said, the legacy of *shtetl* ancestors who hid under their beds in fear of the Cossacks.

As a teenager, I used to clip stories about accidents from newspapers and save them in a manila folder. One story I remember was about a young girl in the Midwest, the teenage daughter of a famous college football coach. On her way home from a school dance one night, she lost control of the car she was driving and hit the highway divider. She was not drunk; the headlights of an oncoming car had temporarily blinded her. She awoke from the wreckage a quadriplegic, unable to walk or breathe on her own. The story talked about her shattered dreams for college and an independent life, and the family's brave attempt to deal with this terrible tragedy. The article ended with a description of her at one of her father's games, watching from the sidelines in a wheelchair connected to a respirator.

Life before the accident, life after the accident. Time in such stories seems to divide itself along those lines. Life before the accident is rich, unpredictable, three-dimensional, spontaneous. Life after the accident is flat, predictable, two-dimensional, monotonous. Did the young girl experience any warning signs or premonitions? I wondered. Was the sky heavy and gray the day of that fateful dance? Did the trees sway in a menacing way? Did she feel a chill along her spine when she said good-bye to her parents that evening?

A stroke is also an accident, a "cerebrovascular accident," to use the medical terminology. Were there any warning signs in my father's case?

Yes, my father had high blood pressure. He also had type two diabetes, which, together with hypertension, created a deadly combination of illnesses that made him a likely candidate for stroke, although I was not at all aware of the danger. He might as well have worn a poster board saying, "Stroke, come get me. I am a walking time bomb."

But, also, no. "Don't worry, Charlie," my father's doctor, Dr. Fox, a respected hypertension specialist, had told him many, many times. "Your heart is healthy, you play tennis, you are active and busy, you take your blood pressure medication every day. You'll be strong as an ox for the next ten years." He had said this even though a computerized axial tomographic, or CAT, scan had shown a narrowing of one of my father's carotid arteries, the one that blocked off during the stroke.

My father had complete faith in Dr. Fox, a man who appreciated a good laugh, who was one of the boys. "Charlie, you've got such a wonderful sense of humor," Dr. Fox used to say. I'm sure the two of them used to slap their knees during those examinations, chuckling at some amusing remark of my father's. "I love that Dr. Fox," my father would tell my mother after one of his visits. "He's such a nice guy."

Dr. Fox visited my father in the hospital just once after the stroke. After he was released, Dr. Fox called a few times, but my father never saw him again.

Why was Dr. Fox so cavalier about my father's health? Why didn't he insist on surgery to cleanse the blocked artery of plaque? I've been told that my father was not a good candidate for this procedure because of his diabetes, but I don't know whether or not that's true.

For many years, my mother, brother, and I blamed Dr. Fox for my father's stroke. But now they're both gone, and recriminations seem a waste of time and energy.

And I wondered, too, if maybe Dr. Fox really had warned my father about his health and advised him to watch his weight and cholesterol, but my father, out of fear and a highly developed mechanism of denial, never told anyone about it.

Over the next few days after my father's stroke I develop a new routine: wake up, get the kids to school, go to the hospital, come home, get dinner ready, help the kids with their homework, get them ready for bed, cry, go to sleep.

My father has been moved out of the ICU into a neurological unit. He drifts in and out of consciousness. Sometimes he says a few words, but his voice is gravelly and difficult to understand. Mostly he sleeps.

My mother, brother, and I don't really understand what is happening. We have no idea what to expect. We walk in circles, completely dazed. We grasp the fact my father is very ill, that he has come near the portals of death, and that his prognosis for recovery is not good. But the gap between awareness and acceptance is very large indeed.

On Saturday night after the stroke, my husband and I go to the hospital to visit him. He is lying shrouded in bed. He opens his eyes for a few seconds when we kiss him, then closes them again. We sit there watching him sleep until suddenly, the ventilator buzzer for the patient in the next bed starts to ring.

We look at each other in alarm. No one comes in. Finally, after what seems to us an eternity, a nurse comes in muttering and shuts off the alarm. "He keeps trying to pull out his tubes," she says to us, as if apologizing for such bad behavior.

We feel sorry for this comatose young man who is hooked up to a respirator next to my father. From the tag on his bed, we learn that his name is Luis. No one ever comes to visit him. My father mentioned that he likes Luis, because Luis doesn't boss him around.

Later that evening, my brother arrives with his friend Arnie, a physician visiting from Boston. Arnie checks my father's bed. "You know, he should be on an air mattress," he says flatly. We stare at him in stunned silence. What is going on? What is he talking about? Why didn't anyone tell us? Don't they take care of stroke patients on this floor? "It's important," he insists. "You don't want your father getting bed sores."

I go running to find a nurse and tell her about the air mattress. "He's on an air mattress," she states with great certainty. After a few minutes I persuade her to come see for herself. She feels the bed. "This is an air mattress, but it hasn't been inflated," she admits. "I'll have to go get a pump." Two hours later, she returns with a pump, inflates the mattress, and we start to breathe once again.

The next day we learn that the air mattress deflated again because of a slow leak. Two more days pass before my father gets a new one.

After we leave the hospital that evening, Arnie takes me aside. "You know," he says, "you should check to see that they remove your father's catheter as soon as possible; it can become infected. Also, you want to make sure they keep track of his bowel movements so that he doesn't become constipated." I stare at him. This is overwhelming. How am I supposed to do all this? Isn't this the nurses' job?

I mention to Arnie that my father complained that sometimes he has trouble sleeping at night because the lights in the room and hallways are always on. "There's something called ICU psychosis," Arnie says. "Sometimes patients become completely disoriented by the lights and they lose track of time." I shake my head. This really is too much.

By now we are standing in the hospital parking lot, which is dark and deserted. My brother has gone to get his car; my husband is at the far end of the lot, helping my mother load flowers from my father's room into her car. Arnie turns to say good-bye. "Hospitals are really dangerous places to be if you're ill," he says. The evening is warm, but suddenly I am chilled to the bone. I know he is not joking.

My father is moved out of Luis's room and onto another floor. His condition has stabilized; he is more alert and stays awake for longer periods, fifteen minutes at a time now instead of five. His voice remains gruff and raspy. The stroke has permanently damaged his vocal cords, and we learn that the old voice is gone forever. His left arm and leg are paralyzed—for the time being, we think. We assume that someday, after physical therapy and rehabilitation, he will walk again, though with a bad limp or shuffle.

My father must have found it difficult to disembark the *Neue Amsterdam* on November 7, 1938, just a few days before Kristallnacht's vandals wrecked synagogues and looted Jewish homes and businesses throughout Germany. An outsider in the New World, a refugee from Hitler's Europe, he barely spoke English. The family's heirlooms—rugs, furniture, paintings—remained in Germany, because all property belonging to Jews had been confiscated by the Nazis. After the Nuremberg Laws were passed in 1935, Jews lost their legal status as German citizens, even though many, my grandfather among them, had fought loyally on behalf of the Kaiser during the First World War.

My grandfather had sequestered his savings in a Dutch bank account; he used the money to bribe a Nazi official to let the family escape. They were three—my grandfather, my father, and my aunt. My father's mother, Flora, had passed away in 1935—but his parents had divorced several years earlier. The only possession of value they took with them was my grandfather's BMW. At least they drove off the boat in style.

My grandfather, Kurt, could not practice as a physician here until he passed the American licensing exams, so he worked as a nurse to support his son and daughter until he could resume his profession. He and my father had a difficult relationship. Kurt was disappointed when my father chose to study accounting rather than medicine; he perceived this as a lack of ambition in his son. When my father graduated from Baruch College—the first in his family to acquire a college degree in America—my grandfather did not attend the ceremony.

Although my father never mentioned it to me, I think he must have mourned the family's decline in status. He insisted he knew Henry Kissinger and Ruth Westheimer, German exiles like himself, from his high school days at P.S. 168 in Washington Heights. He even approached Kissinger once in a Broadway theater before the Secret Service agents could shoo him away. Kissinger was polite but noncommittal, and later, my father admitted he must have gone to school with Walter, the brother, rather than Henry. He was proud that we were distantly related to the director Mike Nichols, who had never once deigned to acknowledge our existence.

I used to think these famous, successful celebrities ignored us because we lived in New Jersey, beyond the pale of civilization. I thought my father had made a big mistake in moving to a development in the suburbs rather than an abode on Park Avenue, an address that would have been far more appropriate for the family of a European émigré.

My father married a woman whose roots were in the Russian *shtetl* and thus completely foreign to his. My mother's parents were poor Lithuanian immigrants looking for a better life in the *Goldene*

Medinah—the Golden Land—around the turn of the century. My grandfather, Philip, a tailor, met my grandmother, Bessie, in Philadelphia when he came to court her sister, Rose. Philip and Bessie fell in love and were married. They raised three children in a one-bedroom apartment on the outskirts of Philadelphia. My grandfather had a shop where he did clothing alterations for fancy Main Line customers and made fur coats, a skill he had learned in the Old Country, where such garments were a necessity rather than a luxury during the long, frigid winters.

My mother grew up envious of the ease and affluence of her Main Line classmates, whose dresses came from the racks of Wanamaker's rather than their mothers' sewing machines, and whose parents spoke English without an accent. During a talk at her local library several years ago, I heard my mother recount to a room full of strangers a story about how she used to help her father make deliveries to his customers, who told them to use the back door. I sat there in dismay, sensing the pain and humiliation those words must have caused.

When I was growing up, I bemoaned our family's anonymity in the suburbs. I fantasized that my parents were deposed royalty, Jewish versions of Nicholas and Alexandra, and that I was a princess, trapped not in a castle with turrets but a split-level ranch.

As a Jew among Christians and the daughter of a German refugee, I felt like an outsider, a foreigner. "Don't tell anyone you're Jewish." Did my parents whisper this to me, or did I just imagine it? Nonetheless, year after year, I was called on by my schoolteachers as the resident Jew to explain the meaning of Hanukkah to my non-Jewish classmates, who argued that I had gotten the better deal in terms of holidays, because Hanukkah meant eight nights of presents, whereas Christmas meant just one.

No, I wanted to tell them. Hanukkah couldn't possibly compete with Christmas, with carols on the radio and wreaths and lights on all the houses; with an evergreen in the school lobby and a massive tree in every town square; with Santa Clauses in department stores, on street corners, on fire trucks parading through town.

Hanukkah isn't about gifts, I wanted to say. It is the story of a miracle, of a vial of oil that burned in a holy temple for eight nights. But in order to tell the story of that astonishing event, I would have had to talk about a king named Nebuchadnezzar, the Maccabee warriors, and an oppressed tribe of people to a room full of puzzled kids for whom the narrative was ancient and just a tad incredible. I couldn't do it; I was too ashamed of being different.

I didn't want to be set apart; I wanted to blend in with everyone else. But I also wanted to be an artist. My mother used to nag me about my dark, unruly hair, which I refused to brush because I felt it made me more bohemian. I resented my parents for forcing me to live a comfortable, middle-class existence when I wanted to be a starving writer and wander the streets of Paris.

I kept these aspirations to myself. My father believed that financial security was the key to happiness, and if I couldn't earn enough money to support a middle-class life, at least I could marry someone who did. I was less certain of my mother's philosophy, beyond the awareness that she was exasperated by my disinterest in clothing and my appearance.

I was my father's daughter. I was stubborn and wanted my own way.

At the age of four, I was ignominiously expelled from Miss June's School of Ballet for refusing to follow her instructions regarding *plié* and *relevé*. By seven, I had become so disruptive by calling out in class that my second-grade teacher, Mrs. Stein, took me aside and told me to write stories after I'd finished my classwork. I was to read these tales to the class during rest period (yes, Virginia, in those days we had rest period after lunch). Thus, I became an author.

I created a series of adventure stories with a toad as protagonist. The stories did not survive, but I was affectionately called Toad for many years by my childhood friend Steven, who died at the age of thirty-five in a civilian car accident in Israel.

I stood in front of the class and read aloud the narratives I had penned while everyone else was working on their list of spelling words. I can still remember the sting of rejection I felt when one day, after a period during which my stories had met with much acclaim, my classmates announced that they did not enjoy the latest installment as much as they had the previous ones.

My father refused to speak German at home, because he said it reminded him of the Nazis. Even so, he maintained a cache of German endearments for my mother and me. He called me *fledermaus* (bat), *schwartze katz* (black cat, because of my hair), *schwalbe* (swallow, as in the bird), and *schaetzle* (little treasure). He called my mother *schnecke,* which means "snail."

"*Schnecke!*" he would holler from their bedroom. "Is my gray suit still at the cleaners?" Or "*Schnecke!* Did you xerox those tax forms yet?" My father would never have admitted it, but he was helpless without my mother. "He can't even boil water," my mother would say, shaking her head, secretly pleased by his dependence on her. Their marriage was a bargain made during earlier times: I will support you and our family if you take care of me.

When I think of my parents' marriage, I am reminded of a passage in the novel *Daughters* by Paule Marshall. The adult daughter, Ursa, leaves her brownstone in Brooklyn to pay a visit to her parents, who live on the Caribbean island where she was born. On an excursion to the mountains, she observes them from the backseat of their car. Studying their profiles, which remind her of engravings on a coin, she realizes she is separate from them, and that their relationship will never be transparent to her because, fundamentally, it is their own private bond.

My parents often fought and argued, and their battles were painful for me, especially during my father's illness. Yet their marriage lasted forty-five years—nearly half a century—and they cared deeply for one another.

A week has passed since the stroke, and my mother, my brother, and I are still confused and disoriented.

Arnie tells me that I should bribe the nurses to take good care of my father. I find myself bristling at his suggestion, because I have always believed that a job well done is its own reward. No, says Arnie. The nurses in this hospital are not bad nurses or bad people. A national shortage of nurses has precipitated a crisis, and many city hospitals, including this one, are seriously understaffed. These nurses are overworked and underpaid, he tells me. They may have begun their jobs with enthusiasm and compassion, but they were not recognized or compensated for their efforts, and they are totally burned out.

I know I should believe him. He trained in a city hospital much like this one, and he knows what he is talking about. But I am reluctant to do something that feels so unethical. Besides, how much money are we talking about? Twenty dollars? Fifty dollars? I have absolutely no idea. I decide to soothe my conscience by bringing in a box of bakery cookies on my next visit.

As soon as I hand the plain cardboard box tied with red-and-white string to the nurse at the nurses' station, I know I have made a mistake. This is not at all what Arnie had in mind; he was talking about cash. As the nurse takes them from me with a desultory thanks, I introduce myself as Charlie's daughter and ask her to take special care of my father. She doesn't bother to look up from her paperwork.

My mother has taken to prowling the halls of the hospital with a notebook and pen. I, too, have a new notebook that I carry with me all the time, even in the car. Everything is so overwhelming, and there are so many questions. The questions give birth to new questions, and those questions spawn other questions, so that the pages are always filling up with unanswered questions. How much will it cost to hire a private-duty nurse for my father? Will he ever walk again? How long will he be in the hospital? When will he go to a rehab center, and how long will he stay there? Will they be able to help him learn how to walk?

And then there are the questions the doctors can't answer: What's going to happen to his accounting practice? Who's going to pay all the bills that are piling up? What will become of him? And what will become of our family?

Before my father's stroke, I had been studying for my qualifying exams for my doctorate in English. Now I can't study anymore. I am too tired to concentrate, and the words in my books are incomprehensible, slithering about meaninglessly on the page. So I put my studies aside and carry my stroke notebook with me instead.

My father is not getting better. He sleeps most of the day; he barely speaks. He can't sit up, can't turn over, can't stand, can't walk.

Sometimes I think that his healthy self has taken a temporary vacation, leaving a shadow self in the bed. I imagine myself running into my healthy father, chatting with the nurses or visiting another patient.

But the healthy father never appears. Each time I visit, I am shocked to see a feeble, immobile, unresponsive man whose hospital ID bracelet bears my father's name.

I am running on empty. I am living two lives, a home life and a hospital life. Neither life seems connected to the other, and neither one seems real. The world is blurry and out of focus. The only time I feel like myself is when I'm driving my car.

When I'm at the hospital, I'm chasing after doctors. If I call them from home before I leave for the hospital, they're not in. I don't leave a message, because I hope to speak to them when I arrive. If I can't find them, I don't leave a message, because I'm not at home in the afternoons and will miss their call. I spend a lot of time and energy planning my strategy for making contact with the neurologist, writing down questions, camping out in front of the elevator, accosting him as soon as he emerges. I feel like a general planning a military campaign.

At home, there is no one to talk to. My kids are too young, and I don't want to burden them with my fears. My husband is busy with work and still grieving for his own father, who passed away three months earlier. My friends assume that since my father hasn't died, he must be getting better.

I can't find the words to tell them he is not better. He is different. He has changed. "Something terrible has happened," I whisper when I'm by myself.

A conundrum has developed at the hospital. The neurologist tells me that my father cannot make any progress toward recovery without physical therapy. The physical therapist tells me that my father is very weak and does not participate in the exercises she tries to do with him. When I tell this to the neurologist, he says, "But the only way he will recover any strength or movement is by doing physical therapy." The situation is exacerbated by the fact that when the physical therapist arrives, my father is often not in his room because he is having a CAT scan, an MRI, or some other diagnostic test.

I speak to the head nurse on my father's floor, who says that it is impossible to coordinate my father's various tests around the physical therapist's visits. The tests take precedence, and their timing is unpredictable.

The therapist says she has a very tight schedule that does not allow her to return to a patient who is not in his or her room when she arrives.

I consider moving into the hospital so that I can coordinate my father's physical therapy appointments around his tests.

Two weeks have passed since the stroke. One day I am visiting my father when a social worker arrives and announces to my mother and me that my father will be discharged from the hospital in a day or two.

My mother and I stare at each other in shock and disbelief. What is she talking about? This is a man who nearly died, and now you're telling us he has to leave? He can't move, can't sit, can't stand, can't walk, can't feed himself, can't go to the bathroom. Where is he supposed to go? Why weren't we told about this earlier?

The social worker says that yes, she is aware that my father has only been in the hospital for two weeks. Yes, she knows he is very sick and weak, but he has passed out of the acute phase of care into what is called the "chronic phase." Medicare no longer pays for chronic hospital care, so he will have to go into a subacute facility—that is, into a nursing home.

Well, this is a shock. I have a horror of nursing homes. All over America, thousands and thousands of men and women are patients in nursing homes. I know this. But I do not want to see my father in a nursing home. I was totally unprepared for this turn of events.

"What about rehab?" we ask her. "What about Kessler or Burke?"

"No," the social worker says. My father has been rejected from local rehab facilities, including the rehab unit in this very hospital. She has faxed them his physical therapy reports, which say he does not participate sufficiently. Rehab hospitals are considered acute-care facilities, and patients need to be strong enough to take part in their rigorous therapy programs. Because my father is not strong, they will not accept him as a patient.

I am enraged. The irony of all this is not lost on me. The doctors at the hospital say that my father needs to do physical therapy in order to regain his strength. But the rehab facilities say he is not strong enough to do physical therapy. Then how, how, is he going to get better?

My mother has started to research nursing homes. She is considering one called Sunnyvale, about fifteen minutes from her house, and she asks me to come look at it with her. I am reluctant to do so, because I've been thinking about going back to studying for my exams. But I want to help, so I agree to go with her.

The lobby is pleasant and tastefully decorated, with rose-colored walls, Monet posters, and reproduction Victorian furniture. The upper floors do not disguise the truth of this place: long, white corridors with room upon room of old, sick people.

The public relations woman who gives the tour shows us the dining room, the recreation room, the small rehabilitation room. We ignore her cheery prattle. In the rehab room she talks about the state-of-the-art this and the new that. We are not impressed. No matter how she tries to gussy up the story, this is still a nursing home. Everyone here is sick and old. There are wheelchairs and walkers everywhere. My father does not belong here. We were not expecting this.

As we leave, my mother bursts into tears. It reminds her of the nursing home where her father died. She feels terribly guilty. But we must find a place for my father. He is not well enough to come home two weeks after a major stroke. He needs round-the-clock nursing care and physical therapy. He needs to regain his strength.

We agree that Sunnyvale will have to do.

I call a woman named Denise. I have known her for years; our kids went to preschool together, but we were never especially close.

Years ago, when I went to pick up my son at her house one afternoon, she showed me the handicapped bathroom she had had built in her basement to accommodate her father, who had suffered a stroke several years earlier. At the time, I paid no attention. The illnesses of parents and older people was a subject better left unspoken, as far as I was concerned, and I had no idea what a stroke was, except that it sounded extremely inconvenient. But right now I am desperate for support, so I call her.

Her father did not go into a nursing home, she tells me on the phone. Medicare was far more generous back in the days before managed care; it paid for her father's entire stay in the hospital, which was six weeks—six weeks—instead of two. He went right from the hospital into Kessler for rehabilitation.

Although I am envious that she did not have to transfer her father into a nursing home, it helps me to talk to her about the experience of stroke. "It's like a death," she says. "You've lost the father you've always known." I find her words comforting. Her ability to articulate the pain of this paradox—the death of a living person—sustains me.

Denise and I meet for lunch. We compare notes over sandwiches at a local café.

"My father was only sixty-five when he had the stroke," she tells me. "It caused a huge crisis for our family. My parents could no longer live in their two-story house with my dad in a wheelchair. My mother realized they would have to move. She decided on Florida because we have relatives there, and she thought the warm weather would be good for both of them. And in Florida, there are so many elderly people that they wouldn't stand out." She pauses. "You know, because of the wheelchair. But it was very hard on both of them. They had lived in their house for more than thirty years and had lots of friends. My father had been president of the synagogue. They were part of the community."

As I listen to her, I realize that I rarely see people in wheelchairs, let alone older people in wheelchairs. Is this true, or is it just that I hadn't been paying attention?

I find myself broaching the subject of finances, even though my mother had warned me not to talk about money with friends. "It's as bad as religion and politics," she once told me. "It's a topic that just breeds resentment." But it is almost impossible to talk about stroke without raising the question of money. I decide to gamble that Denise will understand.

"We were lucky," Denise says. "About a year before my dad's stroke, my parents met with a financial planner and did some long-range estate planning. They're in good shape." She tells me that her parents had purchased a long-term care insurance policy, which covers the cost of a nursing home as well as home health care.

My father has no such insurance policy, and now it's too late to buy one. He thought long-term care insurance was a waste of money. The premiums were very high, and besides, he never thought he would go into a nursing home. "My time will be up on the tennis court," he used to say to us. "You'll see."

In his early sixties, when he would have considered such a purchase, he would have seen long-term care insurance as too expensive, and by the time he was diagnosed with diabetes—when he was in his late sixties—it was too late.

I don't know how to feel about his shortsightedness. A whole new set of unforeseen expenses is now emerging, including the necessity of hiring full-time, live-in help. Wouldn't he have been better off paying the high premiums and having protection?

I have started to sweat. I had always been sheltered from the subject of personal finances; as the daughter of an accountant and the wife of an investment banker, I could afford to be ignorant. Now I can no longer maintain this position. My father is paralyzed and cannot work. My mother does not have any experience in managing their finances. I must now be involved and informed, an active partner in their lives.

Lunch is over. It has taken a lot out of both of us. Denise tells me that our talk has revived some of the painful, intense memories of the early days of her father's stroke. I understand that I, too, am a refugee from my sheltered past. I see that the road ahead will be difficult and fraught with unfamiliar responsibilities.

We hug as we part in the parking lot. We are now sisters in stroke.

My earliest memory of my father is of him teaching me to ski. I was three years old, a young couch potato in training, with no desire to strap wooden slats to my rubber boots and slide down a hill. Nonetheless, my father insisted that I learn.

He took me to a golf course near the house, planted me on top of a knoll that looked like Mount Everest, and commanded me to go down. I sat in the snow and started to cry. Unmoved, he positioned himself farther away, glared at me, and repeated his command: "Go down, Nancy." This time, I went.

The zeal with which my father approached skiing frightened me. I associated it with his childhood in Germany and felt that he wanted me to learn how to ski so that if the Nazis came to New Jersey, I could escape over the mountains, like the von Trapp family in *The Sound of Music*. I was also very anxious to please him and followed him down terrain marked with a black diamond for "Expert" even though I felt each run would be my last. But I went anyway; I descended those steep, difficult slopes and even encouraged my husband and children to learn to ski, knowing my father was proud that his legacy had been handed down to the next generation.

But whether it was because I learned in fear as a child, or because my favorite recreational pastime is reading, I never enjoyed skiing. A few years ago I gave it up completely, without regret.

My father was an enthusiastic, zealous skier. In the fifties, he and his German-born buddies from the Boots and Poles Ski Club in New York would make the endless, winding trek up Route 17 (there was not yet a New York State Thruway) to the Catskills. We have photos of him leaning against the front porches of decrepit ski lodges, his skis and friends beside him, looking perfectly content.

When my father taught us to ski in the sixties, the sport had not yet become popular. There were no condominiums or restaurants at the base of the mountain, no high-speed chairlifts, no clothing made of lightweight microfibers. You laced up your boots and attached them to skis with wire cable bindings, put on a jacket that made you look like the Michelin Man, and hoped not to die or freeze to death in the wilderness.

Later, my father embraced the new equipment, which made the sport much more enjoyable. Buckle boots were warmer and easier to put on. Fiberglass skis with step-in bindings were lighter and faster. Nonetheless, he resisted the changes in clothing, even though the new materials were more wind resistant and less bulky. He thought that stylish skiwear detracted from the integrity of the sport. Skiers had to suffer in order to persevere. I see now that this outlook might have formed the basis of his philosophy of being and existence.

In my father's book, you skied until three o'clock in the afternoon, no matter how cold your toes were. I remember complaining once that my nose was freezing; my father grudgingly let me call it quits early because small white spots were starting to form on my cheeks. One year it was so cold at Mount Mansfield that the chairlift attendants were handing out army blankets to the skiers crazy enough to be out there. Did that deter my father? Not at all. We skied till three that day, too—or at least it felt like we did.

For many years, I carried my father's torch, insisting that the new clothing did not respect the spirit of skiing. I was a lone advocate of the old style of skiwear until, finally, manufacturers stopped making the heavy, bulky stuff, and it was no longer available.

My father was known for forays into the mountains when bad weather threatened to close the roads. One year he packed up our car and headed for Vermont just as the radio announced that a blizzard was causing a state of emergency there. Our neighbors' faces as they crossed the street to watch him load up our car were a study in disbelief.

"You know, we heard that Vermont is closed to all but emergency vehicles," they offered, emphasizing the last two words as they eyed our behemoth Pontiac Starchief.

"Oh, I know," my father replied, impatiently waving away their caution.

I had the uneasy feeling that our Lutheran neighbors had closer ties to God than we did; after all, there were so many more Christians than Jews in the world, which must mean something. I worried that we would be punished for challenging Him, especially at Christmas, His son's birthday. During the trip I kept my mouth clamped shut in the back seat, filled with dread as our car fishtailed along narrow roads flanked by frozen streams and cliffs of ice. But we made it to our destination intact—even though it took more than ten hours—and I uttered a silent prayer of thanks to God for protecting us, the family of infidels.

The day before my father is to be discharged from the hospital to Sunnyvale, Dr. Markowitz, the neurologist who has treated him, comes to say good-bye. I like him; he is kind and compassionate. We shake hands in the hallway, and he tells me that my father's stroke has caused extensive brain damage. In addition to the paralysis in his left arm and leg, there are other symptoms of permanent injury:

Memory. His short-term memory has been affected, which will make abstract thinking and social interaction difficult.

Personality. Stroke often causes major personality shifts, catapulting someone who is gregarious and outgoing into someone who is withdrawn and unfriendly. Frequently stroke victims become hostile and angry, and they cannot control their anger or mood swings.

Depression. Stroke alters brain chemistry, causing stroke victims to become deeply and chronically depressed. The motivational center of the brain is also affected, so that stroke patients are often not motivated to interact with other people or participate in activities, including their own rehabilitation.

These are just some of the problems I should anticipate; there may be others.

I stand there, nodding dumbly. I have become accustomed to hearing bad news.

Sunnyvale is a nightmare. My father is gradually gaining awareness that something dreadful has happened to him. Although he is still weak, he is angry, cursing and shouting at the nurses and the aides when they come into his room. The staff dislike him; they think he is difficult. When I come to visit, he often ignores me. His hostility and silences are unfamiliar and terrifying.

One crisp October morning I decide to take him outside for a breath of fresh air. It is the first time he has been out-of-doors since the stroke four weeks earlier. I drape a windbreaker over his hospital gown as he slumps to the side of his wheelchair.

As soon as I wheel the chair through the front door, I realize I've made a mistake. The cool breeze is too powerful, the autumn sun too bright. He is too frail to enjoy this, and I am overwhelmed by the harsh unfamiliarity of pushing my father in a wheelchair. Still, I decide we should stay out here for at least a little while in an attempt to enjoy the fine weather. I station the chair near the door and stand behind it as my father stares blankly ahead into the parking lot.

A couple gets out of their car. They are good friends of our family; they have known my father since the late forties, when the three of them lived near each other in Washington Heights. The woman places her hand on my father's shoulder. "Be strong, Charlie," she says. "You'll get through this." My father continues to stare ahead in stony silence.

I notice that my head is bobbing up and down in response to his friend's encouragement. Actually I feel like screaming. Inside me now there is a very angry homunculus, an evil little Nancy who hates everyone. My head bobs in order to silence the hateful Nancy who wants to

yell, "Go away! Go away and leave us alone! You can't help us! Don't
you see what has happened here?"

A week later, I visit my father at Sunnyvale, and I tremble as suddenly I understand how ill he has become since the stroke.

He had never been vain about his appearance, the way some men
can be. Still, I am not prepared to see this old man with oatmeal drib-
bling down his chin, stubble all over his face. "Nancy," he rasps. "Go
get the nurse. I need the urinal."

This is why I hate to visit my father. I am afraid I will not find someone in time and he will have an accident and soil himself because of
my incompetence. I go tearing down the corridor and rush up to the
nurses' station. "My father needs an aide, he needs help with the urinal." I am out of breath.

The nurse does not look up from behind the desk. "You'll have to
find the aide assigned to his room. Lucy. She's around here somewhere." My eyes scan the vacant corridors to the right and to the left
of her desk.

"You don't understand," I persist. "It's an emergency. He needs
someone right away." The nurse shrugs. "I'm sorry," she says. "It's the
aide's job. There are two per unit. Your father is not the only patient
here, you know."

The nurses don't like my father. He's demanding. He's not interested
in the needs of other patients. As I turn away, my face prickling in resentment, I spot one of the aides at the far end of the hallway and race
to get her attention before she disappears into someone else's room.

I have decided it's my job to get my father out of Sunnyvale and into
Kessler, which is known for its rehabilitation program. It has become
my *cause célèbre*. I feel as passionate about this as if I'm an ambitious
mother scheming to get her son into Harvard.

Christopher Reeve is a patient at Kessler. I want my father to go
there.

Christopher Reeve's riding accident occurred in May of 1995, and
he entered Kessler around the time my father had the stroke. The two
events have become linked in my mind. When I mention this to people, they say that Christopher Reeve's story is much more tragic than

my father's, because the actor was so young when misfortune struck. Granted, I think, but Christopher Reeve is not my father.

My father keeps getting rejected from Kessler. The social worker at Sunnyvale faxes my father's physical therapy reports to the Kessler admissions people, and they fax back a letter saying they will not admit him. They say he has not made enough progress in rehab, that he is too weak to take part in their program, that the physical therapy services he receives at Sunnyvale are sufficient for his needs. I ask Dr. Markowitz to write a letter on his behalf:

October 6, 1995
Attn: Ms. Victoria Russo
Kessler Rehab Facility

Dear Ms. Russo:
    I was asked to contact you by Ms. Nancy Gerber, the daughter of Charles Frankel. Mr. Frankel has been under my care in the Neurovascular Unit from September 18 through October 6. He suffered a right hemisphere stroke involving portions of the frontal and parietal lobes. He began on a course of physical therapy here and was making some progress. I feel he needs a more comprehensive program and would benefit by an inpatient course in an acute rehabilitation facility.
                                        Sincerely,
                                        Randall Markowitz, M.D.

The letter does not do any good.
    I am beside myself with frustration. I feel in every fiber of my body that my father simply must go to Kessler, that he deserves to go, and that he will not recover unless he goes. Somewhere below the level of rational thought resides a hope that the staff at Kessler will work their magic: they will be able to make him walk.
    I call the admissions office in West Orange several times a week, cajoling, begging, pleading. They are polite but firm. "Your father does not belong here," they say. "He belongs in a subacute facility just like Sunnyvale. We also own several subacute facilities in the area. Perhaps you would like to look into one of those."

One day my aunt comments on my distress. "Why don't you call Kessler and ask them to give you a tour?" she says. "Surely they can't refuse to do that."

This is brilliant, a brainstorm! Without realizing it, I had lost the ability to engage in productive thinking and problem solving. I was so tired, so lost, that I had become like a hamster on a wheel, going over and over the same unyielding ground. My aunt's suggestion is something new, something promising, something I hadn't thought of. I feel exhilarated, powerful.

I phone Kessler in Saddle Brook. Kessler operates three acute facilities—in East Orange, West Orange, and Saddle Brook—and I've heard that the one in Saddle Brook is known for stroke rehabilitation. Denise's father was a patient in Saddle Brook.

Vanessa Stephens, who is in charge of public relations there, is warm and friendly on the phone. "It sounds as though your father could be a candidate for admission," she says to me. "We usually let the staff in West Orange make decisions regarding admissions, but once in a while we bypass them and do our own evaluation. I'll be happy to give you a tour and talk to you about it."

I am elated. I feel hopeful for the first time in weeks.

On a warm Wednesday in early November, my mother and I meet Vanessa Stephens at Kessler for a tour. I am so impatient I can barely contain my anxiety. Fine, everything looks just fine! I want to tell her. Let's dispense with the formalities! When can we have my father transferred here?

My eyes register dull gray hallways, drab rooms, peeling paint. The Saddle Brook facility is in the midst of renovation, and the patients' rooms have not yet been repainted. On the other hand, there is an aura of professionalism, energy, and caring that is missing at Sunnyvale. You can feel it in the air. Never mind the rose-colored lobby at Sunnyvale. This is the place to be! I smile and nod politely during the tour, but I pay little attention to Vanessa's words. I have already made up my mind.

When the tour ends, Vanessa Stephens reaches out to shake my hand. Suddenly the story comes pouring out: the endless faxes back and forth, the phone calls, the pleading, the frustration, the rejections. She listens patiently and thoughtfully. When I finish, she says, "It sounds as though your father belongs here. Have Sunnyvale fax me the physical therapy reports, and I will personally show them to the medical director." A shower of joy explodes inside me. I want to hug her. I want to dance. I race home and phone Sunnyvale. Then I wait on pins and needles to hear from Vanessa.

She calls the next morning. The medical director has reviewed my father's records and wants to assess his condition with a physical examination to be held at Kessler. If the assessment goes well, she will recommend admission.

Oh, rapture! I phone my mother. I phone my brother. I phone my husband. I phone my aunt. I phone the florist and have them send Vanessa Stephens a huge basket of flowers.

When I was young, I read with complete abandon. I especially loved the classic coming-of-age novels about adolescent girls: *Little Women, The Secret Garden, A Tree Grows in Brooklyn*. I admired the plucky, courageous heroines—young girls who didn't always listen to their mothers. Books allowed me space for my own rebellious stirrings; they were a place to experience adventure, to imagine myself a heroine, a leader. Usually I wanted nothing more than to be left alone with a good book. Before I started to read, before I opened the front cover, I would caress the spine, admire the artwork, trace the embossed letters of the jacket with my finger. This ritual would launch me into the solitary pleasures of reading and contemplation. A book was a compass I could use to gauge the moral complexities of the world and my role in it.

If I get my father into Kessler, I will become the heroine of this story.

The assessment takes place the following Wednesday. My brother, Larry, and I wait in the lobby for my father to arrive on a transport van from Sunnyvale. My mother, who has spent every day with my father since he had the stroke, is on the brink of exhaustion, and Larry and I have told her to stay home and rest.

The driver of the van wheels my father through the revolving door into the lobby. This is the first time I've seen him in street clothes since the stroke. He is wearing a jaunty driving cap and a lopsided smile, his mouth forever condemned to sag in the corner. "Hi, *schaetzle*," he greets me. I sense that he is pleased to be the center of attention once again. My brother steers the wheelchair into the examining room while I follow. My palms are sweating.

The white-coated physician introduces himself as Dr. Singh and asks my father a few basic questions. His name. Where he was born. Who the president is. "Again with the president," my father jokes. But he answers all the questions correctly. He is especially proud that he knows Bill Clinton is president. My father is, after all, a committed Democrat.

Then Dr. Singh examines him. He asks him to raise his right arm first. Then his right leg. Then his left arm. "He can't." I jump in before my father can say anything. "It's paralyzed." Dr. Singh nods and proceeds with the examination, stopping now and then to write a few notes in a chart. He checks my father's eyes, listens to his heart, takes his blood pressure. The exam is nearly over, he says. Then he asks my father to tell him what time it is.

I feel my heart stop. This will be very difficult. The stroke has scrambled the nerves in my father's brain, and the act of telling time — once simple, ordinary, and routine — is now a challenge. I barely register what this means as I wait for him to answer.

My father looks up at the white, impersonal face of the clock on the wall. He studies it intently. I hold my breath and watch the needle-like minute hand creep slowly forward. The room is so quiet I can hear the throbbing of my pulse.

Suddenly his face clears. "It's two-twenty!" he announces triumphantly.

Larry and I let out a whoop. This is the right answer! My father has just been accepted into Kessler.

While my father is a patient at Kessler, I am less agitated. The nursing staff is attentive and kind. The physical therapists are highly skilled, and the rehab room is twice as large as the one at Sunnyvale. My father spends over an hour there every morning. But in spite of all his hard work, the paralysis in his left leg and arm shows little improvement.

Then another problem emerges. My father exhibits the symptoms of a swallowing disorder, dysphagia, caused by nerve damage in the esophagus. He cannot chew or swallow properly. We are told he could develop pneumonia if food or liquids enter his lungs.

Kessler has a program to teach stroke patients how to eat so that their lungs stay clear of fluid. Each weekday, lunch is served as a "therapeutic meal," where stroke patients learn new swallowing skills from the director of speech pathology and the staff speech therapists.

One morning, my mother phones me just before 8:00 in the morning while I'm trying to get the kids off to school. She has been with my father every day; she is exhausted, she needs a break. She asks me to visit during the therapeutic lunch today so that my father will have company.

I am annoyed. I have started studying again for my qualifying exams, which I'm planning to take in the spring. I argue with her that it's not necessary to visit my father during meals, especially ones that are supervised. "He's not going to starve, you know," I snap. "Besides, you're entitled to a break to take care of yourself. This is just the beginning of a very long journey." But then I feel ashamed and guilty. My mother has been caring for my father for forty years. How can I expect her to stop now? "I'll go, I'll go," I say irritably.

At Kessler, I wheel my father into the lunchroom. It is a windowless rectangle, with an oblong table in the center. There is no other furniture. Except for the fact that there are no chairs, it looks much like a conference room.

The other patients are wheeled to the table by aides. A few speech therapists lean against the wall. Mrs. Berg, the director of speech pathology, stands at the head of the table and greets the patients as they are rolled in. I dislike her immediately. She strikes me as someone who enjoys being in charge, and I shiver in dread as I wonder how she treats my father.

"Meat loaf and mashed potatoes! Wonderful!" exclaims Mrs. Berg as if this were lunch at Lutece instead of Kessler.

Every step of the meal is carefully choreographed by Mrs. Berg. "Put your fork down in between bites. Chew each bite slowly," she instructs the patients. "Remember, only one bite at a time. Small sips, Helen, please. Small sips!"

There is silence in the room except for Mrs. Berg's directions. I can feel anger rising in my throat. Surely there is a way to conduct these sessions without infantilizing everyone. These are adults, not kindergartners. But the patients don't seem to mind; if they do, they say nothing.

Then Mrs. Berg trains her eyes on my father. "Charles! I've told you not to drink while you have food in your mouth. You could aspirate!"

Charles has a violent coughing spell, and I am torn between wanting to scream at Mrs. Berg for her insensitivity and wanting to yell at my father for his stubbornness.

"Here, Charles," she says, approaching him. "Perhaps you need a little more thickener in your juice. There, that should help." She stirs some white powder from a jar on the table into my father's apple juice, turning the liquid into a thick, glutinous mess. Now say something human, I think. Say you realize this juice is disgusting. You know you wouldn't want to drink it. But Mrs. Berg returns to her place at the head of the table while Charles puts a large forkful of meat loaf in his mouth and starts coughing again.

"Charles!" booms the voice of Mrs. Berg. "You're not listening to me. Really, you are going to make yourself terribly sick."

"Nurse, nurse!" my father calls out, in between coughs.

"The aides are busy now, Charles," says Mrs. Berg. "You'll have to wait until the meal is over."

"I want to leave. Nancy, take me back to my room!" he commands.

What choice do I have? I wheel my father into the hall and place my arm around his shoulder. "Dad, I'm sorry. I think she means well."

My father ignores this and stares down the hall. If he could wheel himself away with his one good arm, he would. But you need both arms to propel yourself in a wheelchair, so he's stuck where he is.

"Take me back to my room," he says again. I push the chair down the hall and find an aide who offers to put him back into bed.

I return to the lunchroom. The meal is over and the room is empty, except for Mrs. Berg, who is collecting her papers. "I'm sorry," I say. "My father is a very proud man."

"There's no need to apologize," she says curtly. "I've seen this kind of thing before. Some people don't realize I'm just trying to do my job."

I bite my lip. What can I say to her? I have failed once again to accomplish anything: I haven't convinced Mrs. Berg to treat my father with more consideration, and I haven't convinced my father to ignore her overbearing manner and focus on what matters to his health.

HELP WANTED

Home care aide needed for stroke patient. Live in Monday through Friday. Duties include wheelchair transfers and meal preparation. Experience, references, and own transportation required.

In preparation for my father's return home from Kessler, my mother has started interviewing home health aides. I offer to help. We arrange to meet at an agency in Passaic that employs women who have just arrived from Poland.

Even though I am only ten miles or so from my home, I find this urban landscape a kind of no-man's-land, menacing and unfamiliar. Abandoned factories hunker alongside the swampy river, their looming facades a reminder of better times for immigrant workers. The industrial area gives way to a depressing neighborhood of small shops and businesses. Many of the storefronts are vacant, the buildings vandalized.

When I arrive at the office of the Kid Gloves agency, on the first floor of a dingy two-story building, I am greeted by a woman whose English in tinged with a slight accent. She tells me that my mother phoned to say she has a flat tire and will be unable to come. I call her at home and ask whether she has any particular questions she would like me to ask the women I'm about to meet. She says she wants to be able to communicate with whomever she hires, and she wants someone who has had experience working as a home health aide.

The first candidate I meet, Barbara, doesn't speak a word of English. The agency woman tells me that in Poland, Barbara was a professional chef. Barbara smiles sadly at me. I try to explain what the position involves—assisting my father with his daily life. Barbara continues to smile. I realize she hasn't understood a word I've said. I turn to the agency woman and tell her, as politely as I can, that my mother wants to hire someone who speaks English. She translates this for Barbara, who gets up and leaves.

I feel as though I've become the immigration inspector at Ellis Island. I say to the woman, as respectfully as I can, "But, you see, my mother needs someone she can talk to. Someone who speaks English like you." She shakes her head. "For what you can pay, you won't find someone who speaks English like I do. These women will work hard.

They are dedicated. They will stay with your family." I decide to speak with the next candidate.

Mira, a young woman in her thirties with slack blond hair, is so nervous that she is shaking. I tell her about the job. She starts speaking in rapid Polish to the agency woman, who says to me, "Please, slow down; you are making her nervous. Ask her some questions about her family." I want to tell the agency woman that these women are making me nervous, too; I am frustrated, my visit has been a waste of time. But I feel sorry for Mira, so I ask her about her family. In halting, fractured English, she tells me about her three young children, who live in Poland with her mother. I am sorry for her troubles, but I cannot help her. I say, as gently as I can, that I'll have to let her know.

By now, the agency woman is as exasperated with me as I am with her. "Your mother and she will learn to communicate," she insists. "In the beginning, they'll use gestures and sign language. Maybe," she laughs, "your mother will even learn Polish."

I mull this over as the woman leaves to make some phone calls. There is a photograph of Pope John Paul II on the wall, and I think about Poland's history of anti-Semitism and wonder how these women feel about Jews. But, matters of religion aside, they do not have experience working with invalids.

It's time for me to go. I thank the agency woman for her time and assistance.

As I leave, I see Mira sitting huddled on a chair in the lobby, looking like one of Emma Lazarus's silent masses. Her eyes avoid mine, but I silently wish her luck. I hope she will find good fortune in the New World.

The day before my father's discharge from Kessler, the neurologist comes to say good-bye. My father has been a patient here for about four weeks, which is the maximum stay allowed by Medicare. His insurance coverage has run out, so his time is up. Such is the way health care decisions are made nowadays. My brother has tried writing a letter, but to no avail.

The doctor and I chat for a few minutes outside my father's room. "I'm sorry we couldn't help your father. The paralysis is just too dense," he says. Although there will not be any return of mobility in his left arm or leg, he tells me there may be some improvement in speech and memory over the next few months.

"What about TPA?" I ask him, realizing the question is merely rhetorical at this point. "Do you think if he had been given TPA he would not have had the second stroke?" TPA, tissue plasminogen activator, is a clot-dissolving drug that must be administered within three hours of the onset of a stroke such as my father's, one caused by a clot that blocks blood flow to the brain. I had been following stories about this medication in the *New York Times*, and it seemed to minimize brain damage if administered properly.

"TPA is a dangerous drug," he says. "If a stroke is caused by a hemorrhage rather than a clot, TPA could kill the patient. It can't be administered until the results of a CAT scan are in. Besides," he added, "most doctors don't like to use it because the FDA hasn't approved it for use with stroke victims. It's mostly given to cardiac patients."

Recently I read that the Food and Drug Administration has ruled that the manufacturer of TPA can advertise and market the drug as a treatment for strokes.

Three months after my father's stroke, he returns home. He has spent the last twelve weeks in a hospital, nursing home, and rehabilitation center.

My mother has prepared the house for him. A local builder has constructed a wooden ramp leading from the garage into the kitchen for his new wheelchair. The bathroom has been modified, with a wider door and metal grab bars around the toilet and the tub. The house looks pretty much the same as it has for the past forty years. But the modifications clearly mark it as the residence of a handicapped person.

My brother and I are at the house with my mother when the van from Kessler arrives. There is also an aide, Janice, who will be living with my parents now.

My voice is brimming with false cheer as my father is wheeled up the ramp. "Dad, it's so good to have you home!" But I can't go on; I turn away. Janice pulls me aside as the procession continues into the living room. "You mustn't break down in front of your father," she admonishes. "You must be brave for him." I know she's right, so I lock myself in the bathroom where the walls muffle my sobs.

Part Two

AFTERMATH

I used to wonder about my father's childhood in prewar Germany. Sometimes I asked him to tell me about it, but he would not, at least not in any detail.

Once I was home on a break from college and was on my way to work with him, where I was being paid a nominal wage to address envelopes for a party given by one of his clients.

"What was it like when the Nazis came to power?" I asked.

"I've told you before I don't want to talk about that," he muttered, waving his right arm around while his left gripped the steering wheel.

"Please," I wheedled. But I could tell from his tone and gestures that my pleas were futile.

After my father died, I asked my aunt, his sister, Ruth, to tell me their story:

"We were born in Frankfurt, and we stayed there until 1927, when we moved to Stuttgart with our mother. I was seven, and Charlie was five.

"My uncle, Louie Landauer—he was my mother's brother, a rich man, a big shot, he ran the whole family—came to take my mother, Flora, to Stuttgart with him. My mother was unhappily married. My father was fooling around with other women, and he didn't make any bones about it, either. My mother didn't want to leave, because she loved my father, and she would have stayed forever, but I think she had a mental breakdown. Because that's when Uncle Louie showed up and said, 'We're taking your mother to Stuttgart, and you children are coming, and don't talk in the train because your mother is very upset.' I remember that part—*don't talk in the train*.

"We were children, and we had no idea what was happening. We went to my grandmother's house, and my mother went into some kind of rest home for a year. It was run by a Dr. Mann; I remember his name. After she came back, we found an apartment. We lived in Stuttgart until 1935. That's when our mother died, three months before Charlie became *bar mitzvah*. And then a few months after that, our grandmother died. So we went back to Frankfurt to live with my father and his new wife.

"Hilde Flesch. I hated her from the moment I met her. She had three children from her first marriage, and they were nicer than she was. She was divorced, too, like my father. And after that came Hitler.

"She saved our lives. She came to the United States before our father did, and because she was living here, we were able to get out. When she came to pick us up on the dock, she said to my father, 'You have a choice. You can either live with me or live with your children.' He picked us. Can you believe it?

"I became the *hausfrau*. I did all the cleaning and cooking. But your father moved out and went to live with our aunt, my mother's sister, because he didn't get along with our father.

"Neither of us liked to talk about our childhood, because it was so horrible."

My grandmother, Flora Landauer, died of complications from strep throat. In 1935, penicillin was not available. I tried to imagine the sadness of her life by writing a poem:

"*Kaddish* for Flora"

Remember her name.
Flora Landauer.
A circle of gray stones.
Flora Landauer.
Grandmother, I never knew you.
Flora Landauer, Flora Landauer.

Flora, you died before
I was born.
Strep throat, it was nothing, they said.
Nothing.
I think I look like you—
Dark hair, sad smile.
I see you sitting by the fire,
The room full of shadows.

Flora, your name haunts
My dreams.
Every night you visit me,
A little girl in a white frock,
With ribbons that dance in the wind.
You hold out your arms:
"Let's play."
You belong to me—
My sister, my friend.

When I was twelve, I was given an assignment in school to write an oral history of an immigrant. I decided to interview my father. That's when I first heard about my grandfather's BMW.

I told my father that I couldn't interview him because real immigrants were poor. He assured me that, in spite of the BMW, he and his family had had no money when they came to this country. Everything they owned had been left behind.

I was too young at the time to understand that deprivation can be emotional as well as material.

He was not a talkative subject for an interview, having buried the memories of his past beneath years of repression. I ended up interviewing my mother's mother, my grandmother Bessie, who remembered her passage across the ocean alone, in steerage, on a vessel that left Russia for Philadelphia. This, I felt, was a more authentic narrative.

Before adolescence made moments of intimacy between father and daughter taboo, I used to sit in the bathroom and keep my father company while he shaved. We were both in our undershirts. We had a favorite game: I pretended to be Cassius Clay and he was Sonny Liston.

Or I was John Glenn and he was Alan Shepard. I have no real memory of what we said. My father lived in the public world of work and events, whereas I knew only the child's world of play and television cartoons. But the idea was to pretend:

"Hi, Cassius."

"Hi, Sonny. What are you doing?"

"Getting ready to go to work. What about you?"

We loved Alan Sherman songs—not just "Hello Mudda, Hello Fadda" but also lesser-known tunes such as "I See Bones" and "You Went the Wrong Way, Old King Louie."

We both liked to eat. My father was a *fresser*, the Yiddish word for "eater," and so was I. We enjoyed sitting down on Saturdays and Sundays for lunch at my mother's table, on which she had assembled a smorgasbord of German and Jewish favorites: herring in cream sauce, tongue and other smoked meats, whitefish or kippered salmon, pickles, rye bread, lettuce, and tomatoes—all arranged on numerous small plates. Because of the variety, these luncheons had achieved quite a reputation among their friends and my father's tennis partners, who sometimes asked for invitations to join us.

I was my father's partner in food. I couldn't stand any of the fishy stuff, but I relished the cold cuts and also a hard, stringy German version of beef jerky called *landieger*. Sometimes for dessert there was *lebkuchen* (which I didn't like) and *linzertorte* (which I did).

Lunch has now become an ordeal. Once in a while I drive up on Sundays. It's a forty-five-minute trip to my parents' house—time spent away from my own family—but somehow, the time I spend in the car "doesn't count" as part of the visit.

As soon as I get there, I want to leave. It's painful to watch as the aide cuts up meat and vegetables for my father. Meals are no longer social occasions, because my father cannot eat and carry on a conversation at the same time. During meals, he is unable to negotiate the art of talking with the necessity of eating. Since the stroke, he concentrates on chewing and swallowing. Perhaps Mrs. Berg's instructions were useful, after all.

These lunches are a vivid reminder of how much has been lost. They are a unique form of torture.

I don't like to go out to dinner with my father, either.

One evening my husband and kids and I join my parents and brother at a tavern near my parents' house. I have called ahead to ask whether the restrooms are accessible. They say yes.

Many restaurants believe that restrooms are accessible if they are located on the same level as the tables. That's not so. There are specific requirements: the stall must be wide enough to accommodate a wheelchair and must be equipped with metal grab bars.

After the meal, my father asks to be taken to the men's room. The aide takes him. This arrangement upsets me—that there is a woman in the men's room—but the reverse—my father in the women's room—is no better. My father is gone for a long time. After a while, my brother goes in to see if they need help. When he doesn't return, my husband goes in to check. When the waitress comes to see if we would like to order dessert, I tell her that four out of eight people are in the men's room.

It turns out that my father got stuck in the stall. When he returns to the table, he is irritable and exhausted. He wants to go home.

I tell my mother I will no longer eat out with them. My mother says, "We can't be prisoners. This is the way things are now."

They continue to eat out at places like Charlie Brown's and the diner and a local Italian place, but I refuse to join them.

When my father came home from Kessler in December, I started studying for my oral exams in earnest. The exam was scheduled for mid-May.

The adviser of my orals committee suggested I make an index card for each text on my four reading lists: the major novels of Edith Wharton, feminist criticism and motherhood, twentieth-century American literature, and the female *bildungsroman*. Because there were more than thirty titles on each list, I had to familiarize myself with over 120 books and articles, at least to the extent that I could discuss some of them intelligently with the members of my orals committee. Naturally, it is impossible to discuss so many texts in the span of two hours, but the idea is to be an informed discussant in each of the four categories. It was an enormous amount of work, and I set out my cards and my lists with grim determination to study three hours every morning, without answering the telephone.

At first I order caller ID, so that I can see who is calling and decide whether or not I want to take the call. After a while, this process becomes distracting, and I decide to stop answering the phone altogether. But the subtext of my studies is my father's illness, and I worry every day about my parents and how they are adjusting to their new life post-stroke.

My father and mother are struggling. They are facing enormous losses for which they are completely unprepared:

Role reversal. For the first time in their forty-year marriage, my father is dependent on my mother. He used to be in charge of all financial decisions, investments, planning. Now he can't even balance a checkbook.

Identity. My father was working when he had the stroke. Like many men, his identity was entirely bound up with his work, an accounting practice he had established by himself after college. Some of his clients had been friends of our family for nearly fifty years. Now the practice he had called his own and worked his entire life to build has collapsed. The clients have scattered and hired new accountants.

Social life. My parents were sociable people. They enjoyed concerts, movies, restaurants, dinners with friends. Such diversions have now shifted from the category of pleasure to burden. There are a host of variables that make planning difficult: wheelchair access, handicapped restrooms, and whether my father will feel up to going out.

My father had a large group of acquaintances from his involvement with the synagogue and B'nai B'rith, a Jewish men's organization devoted to social causes; UJA (United Jewish Appeal, which raises funds for Israel); tennis; and bridge. Slowly, these people stop coming by. They find it difficult to see my father after the stroke. He is not the Charlie they once knew. It's too painful; it reminds them of their own frailty and mortality. Visitors stop paying calls. The telephone is silent. My father's social circle contracts.

Travel. My parents loved traveling. They were at their best with each other on vacation, when the stresses of home life were removed.

They had been to Israel, Scandinavia, Alaska, the National Parks; they had been in the middle of planning a trip to Italy.

Now, travel is out of the question. My father is a very sick man. Now his itinerary consists of visits to neurologists, endocrinologists, cardiologists, dermatologists, ophthalmologists, psychologists.

Autonomy. My father loved to drive. Cars were a symbol of his self-worth. Right before the stroke he had purchased a brand-new, gleaming Oldsmobile, the car of his retirement. Now it sits in the driveway, a useless white elephant.

Whatever I know—and it is not much—I know my father will never drive again. Even handicapped people need both arms to drive. Even handicapped people must pass an eye test.

My mother hires home health aides to take care of him. My father cannot be left alone in the house. Once he tried to pull himself out of the wheelchair using the legs of a glass étagère. At first he does not fully understand the magnitude of his disability.

Each week two different women come to live with my parents, one during the weekdays, another during weekends. Because the cost of hiring an aide through an agency is very expensive—about $150.00 per day—my mother employs women she finds on her own through ads in the local newspapers.

The aides keep quitting. Janice stayed a few months, then quit. A succession of women has followed her.

Sometimes they are pleasant. Sometimes they don't speak English. Sometimes they refuse to administer insulin, saying they aren't supposed to give injections. Sometimes they argue with my mother, saying they have their own way of doing things. Sometimes they don't show up for work, leaving my mother to make frantic phone calls to other names she has collected along the way. Sometimes, when I come to visit, they confide to me that my father is lovely but my mother difficult, or that my father is difficult and my mother bossy.

My mother employs full-time, live-in help for five years. My father's illness consumes nearly half his savings. It would have been far less expensive to pay the yearly premiums for long-term care insurance. He took a gamble that he'd never need it, and he lost.

A few weeks after my father comes home, it becomes evident that he is no longer the *paterfamilias*. He is neither in charge of himself nor the family.

He needs assistance with the simplest of daily tasks. Opening a tube of toothpaste. Buttoning his shirt. Cutting his food. He cannot dress, shave, relieve himself, push his chair to the kitchen.

In those first few months at home, my mother, brother, and I—even my husband, for whom my father was a kind of surrogate father figure—wished to restore him to his former position of authority. His dependence on all of us was difficult to bear.

We make an appointment to see a psychotherapist, a German-Jewish refugee like my father. She is a woman in her late sixties named Ilse Wolff.

At the consultation in her office, Ilse sits in a chair next to my father. My mother, brother, and I sit facing them on a leather couch. This arrangement seems highly symbolic to me, an alliance of "us" against "them," with Ilse my father's voice and advocate.

"This man needs hope," Ilse announces while my father nods in agreement. Why does she speak about him in the third person, as if he's not there, I wonder.

"What are your hopes, Charles?" she asks, turning toward my father.

"That I will one day walk again," declares my father.

"That's not possible," I say, the voice of reason. "He's paralyzed." So I do the same thing she does, apparently—talk about my father in the third person, as if he's not there.

"This is a metaphor!" Ilse shouts at me as though I am an idiot, or a child. "He knows he will not walk, literally. Walking is a metaphor for how he sees the future. The idea gives him hope!"

I shake my head. I do not agree that walking is a metaphor. My father talks about walking, dreams about walking, envies those who are walking. When the physical therapist comes for home visits, he attempts to get out of his wheelchair and walk. This involves a charade in which the therapist holds him upright on both sides while my father manages to shuffle forward a few feet. This is not walking. It is too painful to watch.

I think my father is pleased that Ilse has stood up to us, the unbelievers. It's now time to discuss other ideas. She suggests that we move my father's desk, which is upstairs in the den, downstairs to his sick room. This will remind him of who he is, she says.

I think she's crazy. The desk is solid oak and must weigh several hundred pounds. Besides, how will an empty surface give him hope? He can no longer concentrate on taxes and W2 forms, and besides, he no longer has any clients or accounting practice to attend to.

"It's a metaphor," says Ilse, annoyed by my skepticism.

I am a literary critic, I want to tell her, and I understand the power of metaphors. But not everything is a metaphor. Some things are what they appear to be. My father wants to walk. The desk is useless. Apparently, I am my father's daughter, after all—literal and pragmatic.

My mother hires a handyman to move the massive desk into my father's room, where it sits in a corner, a reminder of futility. After a while, we forget it's even there.

My brother, my husband, and I are sitting in the conference room of an elder care attorney, a woman of impressive credentials—she is head of the state bar association section on elder care law—about my age. My parents' savings are dwindling at an alarming rate because of their new, unforeseen expenses—the high cost of live-in help and medications. My brother has arranged this meeting to see what can be done to help them.

The elder care attorney advises us to transfer the majority of my parents' assets into a trust, of which Larry and I would be the executors. If my father should have to go into a nursing home, she points out, such a step will allow him to become eligible for Medicaid more quickly. Nursing homes cost between $50,000 and $100,000 per year, she says. Three years after the transfer of assets, Medicaid will pay for a nursing home if an individual can demonstrate that he or she is indigent.

I have difficulty following the thread of her argument. My brother, an attorney, and my husband, a bond trader, are more comfortable with these issues. My brother points out that my father will be very upset when asked to give up control over his life-savings. He is already depressed by his physical condition. A family trust over which he has no authority will seal the lid on his feelings of helplessness and diminishment.

The elder care attorney is sympathetic to our distress but advises us to move forward. "If you don't," she says, "you may find yourself with two parents on Medicaid instead of one." My brother volunteers to take charge of the discussions with my father, for which I am deeply grateful.

My mother and I are arguing over the phone. The newest replacement in a long line of weekend aides has just quit, and my mother has asked me to help her hire someone new. I tell her I am willing to make some initial calls, but I am busy with my two kids and don't have time to do interviews with her. She becomes angry and says I don't do enough to help. "You're so self-involved," she tells me. I hang up on her. A few minutes later she calls back to apologize.

Sometimes I cannot concentrate on my studies. One day, I put my books aside and pick up the phone book. I call every social service agency I can find. Bergen County Office of the Disabled. Caregivers of the Disabled and Elderly. Catholic Community Services (they are ecumenical, and I am desperate). Division of Senior Services. Family Services of Bergen County. Jewish Community Center of the Palisades. Jewish Family Services. Outpatient services at Pascack Valley Hospital, Hackensack Hospital, Holy Name Hospital, Valley Hospital.

These agencies provide a variety of services. Assessment and care plan management. Support groups for caregivers. Counseling. Transportation. Poststroke groups for patients. Meals-on-Wheels. Volunteers who visit shut-ins like my father.

The information is overwhelming, the people I speak to sympathetic and kind. Three hours later, I'm no better off than before. My mother has already met with a geriatric care manager, who is in charge of our "case" and is in the process of preparing a care plan. My mother knows about caregiver support groups and has agreed to give one a try when she feels less overwhelmed. She also has a list of psychotherapists. The county transport van, which could relieve her of some of the endless driving to doctors, must be reserved well in advance, which is not practical at the moment, given the instability of my father's condition. The aide cooks once in a while, and between my mother's meals and takeout, they don't need Meals-on-Wheels.

What our family needs is not listed in the phone book. I don't know what we need. A miracle, maybe.

I decide my mother should go to a support group. I recently found my notes, jotted on a set of xeroxed papers sent to me by a social worker at Hackensack Medical Center, listing support groups near her house.

There are many, sponsored by organizations like the American Red Cross, Caregivers to the Elderly, Bergen County Adult Day Care Center, Bergen Pines Hospital, Pascack Valley Hospital. Most are intended for people who care for Alzheimer's patients. Luckily, my mother makes a connection with a group sponsored by the Well Spouse Foundation, where she is able to find women who understand her anguish.

My father tries going to a poststroke group that meets weekly near their house. He says it's filled with "water heads," his expression for people who can't speak because of aphasia and other communication disorders. I can't say I blame him for being so judgmental. There is nothing wrong with my father's mind. He wants company and intellectual stimulation; he is lonely and isolated. He doesn't want to go to a place where everyone is nodding off in their wheelchairs. The group only makes him more depressed.

There are so many agencies, and yet none seems to offer services that would alleviate my father's loneliness or my mother's anxiety. It's like going to a banquet only to find that the table is laden with food that has spoiled.

I decide to join a caregivers' support group sponsored by the National Council of Jewish Women, for women regardless of religion or faith. I don't know whether I am considered a caregiver or not—technically, my mother is the full-time caregiver. What does that make me? The part-time assistant?

We are a small group of six women, who range in age from midthirties to early sixties. I am the only one among them whose parents are both living. These women see themselves as caregivers, because there is no spouse to assume that role, whereas I am unsure whether or not I can claim that title. I see myself as a dutiful daughter, but in this I am not alone. All of us are dutiful daughters without the authority to convince our parents to do things they don't want to do. These are our parents, after all, not our children.

I don't feel I have much else in common with these women. Their issues differ from mine: how to tell if a father in his eighties is still a safe driver, how to convince a frail mother to sell her home and move into an assisted-living apartment. One woman in her early sixties describes her frustrations with her eighty-five-year-old mother, who is living with her. "Never let your mother move in with you!" she declares.

The women listen helplessly as I voice my grief. They shake their heads and say they wish they had some answers. They say they think I am worse off than they are. I appreciate their compassion and support, but I feel guilty that I have no energy to return it.

During one meeting I describe the powerlessness I feel in the face of my father's illness. One woman suggests my father try listening to books on tape. What about prayer? offers another. She tells the story of a friend, completely bedridden, who is sustained by her faith. The women discuss this response. "You can't just tell a person to pray," I say. "The impulse must come from within."

I become impatient with people's suggestions and advice, even though they are only trying to be helpful. Really, there is nothing to say, except "I'm sorry."

After a few weeks, I decide to leave the group.

My father was not a religious man. I'm not sure if he believed in God; I suspect that he didn't. Although we never spoke about it, I imagine that he wondered why God turned his face away from the Jews when Hitler took control of Germany.

Nonetheless, he was passionately committed to Jewish continuity and tradition and to the future of Israel. In addition to his committee work for the synagogue and B'nai B'rith, he participated for many years in raising money for Israel through United Jewish Appeal. He was honored for his work by a gala dinner.

My parents gave me the middle name Faith. I have always been proud of this name; when I was a child, I wanted to drop my first name—there were just too many Nancy's around—and become Faith. As I grew, I became aware of the advantages of having a hidden name, like a talisman. I am a person of faith, although not necessarily the conventional kind. Rather, I believe that human beings are interconnected by our shared humanity, and that recognizing and honoring this connection will eventually lead to *tikkun olam,* repair of the world. Call it karma, call it God, call it naive, call it what you will.

My father felt that existence was made up of what you could see and touch in front of you, and that was that. We never had conversations about spirituality, or the nature of the divine, or what it meant to be Jewish. We would not have felt comfortable discussing such topics.

I try to describe my parents' struggles to an acquaintance, who tells me the following story about her friend Tracy's parents:

Tracy's mother, who is in her late sixties, starts to develop a form of dementia. In response to the demands of caring for his wife, Tracy's father becomes depressed, starts drinking, and never tells his doctor, who is treating him for hypertension. The combination of alcohol and medication leads to a stroke on the left side of the brain (my father's stroke was on the right side)—the sphere that controls speech and memory—so that Tracy's father now has a kind of dementia as well.

Both parents are sent to the locked psychiatric ward of a nursing home, where, although they don't live in the same room (no cohabitation allowed in nursing homes, not even for spouses), they see each other all the time. Reportedly, both are doing well.

I recount this anecdote to another friend of mine, asking her which situation is worse, that of Tracy's parents or that of my parents. My friend says my parents' situation is worse, because they are keenly aware of their suffering and Tracy's parents are not.

This is true. It is also true that in Tracy's case, both her father and her mother are being taken care of. Nonetheless, I imagine that as daughters, Tracy and I are suffering equally.

I am told that Tracy and her brother argued all the time about their parents' care and stopped speaking to each other. Her brother moved from New York City to Texas, and the two lost contact.

My brother and I argue, too, especially about which one of us is more involved in our parents' lives. My brother says I don't visit enough. I try to explain that I feel like a piece of saltwater taffy, stretched to the breaking point between my parents and my children. "I have kids," I tell him.

"You use that as an excuse," he says. He is not a parent, and I don't think he understands how I feel.

Nonetheless, I hope my brother doesn't move to Texas. He is doing as much as he can, and I don't want to be alone in all this.

On the other hand, I am seriously considering a move to Tibet.

One day I call home and my invalid father answers the phone. "Hello, *schaetzle*," he says. "I want you to know that I'm thinking of divorcing your mother."

Now that's a real conversation stopper. "Dad," I say, trying to remain calm, "do you really think that's a good idea? I know you and Mom are under a lot of stress right now, but what's going to happen to you if you divorce?"

"Your mother can be very difficult," he replies.

"Well, so can you!" I say, although I feel guilty about giving a sick man a dose of reality therapy. Then I hear the clattering of pots and pans in the background, and suddenly I become suspicious. "Dad, where are you right now?" I ask.

"In the kitchen."

"And where's Mom?"

"In the kitchen."

"So you're telling me you want a divorce right in front of her?"

"Yes."

Just as I thought. This little melodrama has been staged for my benefit, to remind me I'm the arbitrator in their struggle to redefine their relationship.

I can hear the kettle whistling and my mother telling my father that his tea is ready.

I can't find the words to describe my feelings. Ordinary language is not sufficient; I need a new lexicon of paradox, oxymoron, disjunction.

People ask me how my father is doing; I open my hands in despair. "He's alive," I want to say, "but he has lost his life. Same thing for my mother." But instead I say, "About the same."

Denise tells me that her mother still cannot accept the radical alteration in the man she married, even though it has been ten years since her father's stroke.

"When I see him, I expect to see him as he was before," her mother tells Denise. "Sometimes I look at him and ask myself, what the hell happened to him?"

Denise says she thinks of her father as two different people, the old one and the new one.

I know exactly what she means. It is not merely the change in physical appearance—the slackness in the face, the withered arm and leg, the raspy voice. I could adapt to such alterations; indeed, people often tell me how well my father looks, all things considered. The psychological crippling of personality is much more profound, because it's on the inside rather than the outside. My father as I knew him is gone. In his place is an angry double.

Of course he is angry. Who wouldn't be angry? He is living with irremediable losses. He's cooped up in the house every day, surrounded by reminders of his former, healthy life.

I understand his anger, but that doesn't mean it's easy to take when it's directed at me.

In May 1996, I take my qualifying exams and pass them. Three weeks later I submit a proposal for my dissertation, which is approved.

At the end of the month, my husband and I take a trip to Paris to celebrate my fortieth birthday and the passing of my exams. In Paris, I am exhausted and irritable. Jet lag follows me like a shadow. Our hotel room on the Left Bank is dark and cramped. I can't speak French well anymore. The foreignness of the city unnerves me.

At dinner one night at Le Pré Catalan, an exceedingly pricey restaurant in the Bois de Boulogne, tears run down my face as I think about my father and how much he loved to travel and that he never will again. I tell my husband I want to go home.

During one of my Sunday visits to my parents' house, I encounter the rabbi from their synagogue, who has become a good friend since my father's stroke. He was the rabbi when I became *bat mitzvah*, and he also performed the wedding ceremony when I married, so I have known him a long time. He tells me he wishes my father had more interests, more diversions. "The only thing he does, as far as I can tell, is listen to classical music on his Bose radio. I am glad he enjoys music, but I am wondering if that's enough."

In theory, I agree.

When my father came home from Kessler, he made a valiant attempt to reclaim lost parts of his life. He went to duplicate bridge in his wheelchair, but the damage to his short-term memory meant he couldn't remember what hands had been played. He tried going to the movies, but diabetic retinopathy was stealing his eyesight. Concerts are out, because he fatigues easily.

So the world has narrowed to his Bose radio.

A kind friend, a man who had been a musician, keeps my father's CD tower well stocked with Beethoven and Mozart. My aunt gives him a CD of the comedy of Mike Nichols and Elaine May. I give him a CD of Jerry Seinfeld.

I try reading to him. On one of my visits, I bring Doris Kearns Goodwin's memoir, *Wait Till Next Year.* He likes Doris Kearns Goodwin; he is familiar with her as a television commentator for the Clinton-Dole presidential race.

The reading does not go well. He tires easily and seems to have difficulty following the narrative, so I drop the project.

Later I realize he was not interested in her words. What he liked was the sound of my voice.

About two years into my father's illness, the question of a nursing home begins to rear its ugly head. My mother's endurance is flagging. Although she has finally found a reliable young woman to live in and take care of my father during the week, she still has not found a regular aide for the weekends.

My father's condition is deteriorating. He is growing weaker and spends almost all his time in bed. My mother worries that she will not be able to care for him properly at home. Her own health is also at risk. A few weeks ago she fell on an icy sidewalk, and she has not gone for the physical therapy she needs. Her shoulder is not healing properly.

Erica, a social worker and geriatric case manager with whom my mother has been working, said that neglecting one's own health is common for full-time caregivers, who devote all their energy to caring for the patient. Erica believes that my father belongs in a nursing home. She has proposed a "family meeting" to discuss the issue.

My brother, my father, and I are seated with Erica around the kitchen table at my parents' house. At Erica's suggestion, my mother is not in the room with us, although she is somewhere in the house.

Erica begins the meeting slowly, asking my father general questions about his health—how he feels about his illness, whether he feels he is making progress toward recovery, how he thinks his situation affects his wife. Underneath the table I am drumming my knees: let's stop all this procrastination and get to the point already!

And then suddenly it's out there, dangling in the air like a hideous dead fish: "Charles, would you be willing to go into a nursing home?"

Charles says, "I've worked all my life for my family. *This* is my home."

Erica tries a different line. "Your kids," she asks. "Do you think they love you?"

"Yes," says my father.

"And do you think they want what's best for you?"

"Yes," says my father.

"And do you think it's their duty to take care of you?"

My father hesitates; he senses she is trying to trap him into saying that if my mother can't take care of him, one of us should. I am certain he believes this, even though we would lose our lives if we were to take on the responsibility of his care. But he is also smart enough to know that Erica would not approve of such an arrangement. Finally he says, "If they love me, they will want what's best for me."

I sigh in exasperation. Of course I want what's best for my father. But what happens when those needs don't mesh with what's best for my mother?

We've been circling around each other for over an hour, and I've had enough. The meeting is finished, and nothing has been resolved.

Months pass. Long days of silence. I am working on my dissertation —a study of the figure of the mother as artist in contemporary American fiction. I have been in graduate school for nine years, and ironically, writing the dissertation is the most satisfying part of the process, even though I am often filled with worry and self-doubt. Stressful as it is, graduate school keeps me going. It's my work, and it reminds me that I have a life outside my father's illness.

I feel guilty that I don't visit enough.

One Sunday afternoon I visit my father. The house is quiet. My mother has gone to see a movie, a rare event for her. The aide is resting in my old bedroom. My father is napping in his room. It's hard to tell if he's really asleep or just shutting out the world.

I pull up a chair next to his bed and watch him. After a few moments he opens his eyes. "Hi, *schaetzle*," he murmurs. He smiles his sad, lopsided smile.

"Hi, Dad. How are you?"

"OK," he answers.

He is in a peaceful mood. I listen for sounds of life outside — wind in the trees, the song of birds. There is nothing. It is absolutely, utterly still. It's as though the neighborhood is resting, too.

Mentally I scroll through the list of topics I've come prepared to talk about, but the quiet is so soothing I don't want to shatter it with small talk.

Finally I lay my head on my father's chest and he strokes my hair, as he did when I was a child. Tears blanket my cheeks. For a brief moment, he's my father again.

On October 24, 1998, my son Josh is called to the Torah as a *bar mitzvah*, a son of the commandments.

This is a big event, because Josh is my father's first grandchild.

My mother and I debate the logistics of the day. We decide to hire a private driver who will take my father back to my house with the aide after the three-hour service is over. The driver will wait while he rests for an hour, then take him to the reception. He will then return after two hours to take my father back home.

The day before the ceremony I go to the synagogue to check on last-minute details, the *bimah* (podium) flowers, the wine and challah for *kiddush*. The secretary tells me the elevator from the first floor to the sanctuary upstairs has just broken. I tell her that it simply must be fixed by the end of the day because my father is in a wheelchair. She asks me whether my father can't be lifted in his chair up the eight or so stone steps in front of the building.

I don't lose my temper. I want to, but what I really want is for the elevator to be repaired. I try as patiently as I can to explain that my father and the chair together weigh probably 180 pounds and that I don't want my father to become a spectacle as he is carried up those steps.

At five o'clock Friday evening, as the office is closing for Sabbath, I get a call that the elevator is working.

I don't remember much about the ceremony. I am overcome with emotion as I sit next to Bobby, my husband, and my son Adam, listening to Josh chant his Torah portion with grace and poise. Because my father cannot get up the stairs to the *bimah*, the rabbi brings the Torah down to where he sits in the front pew, so that he can touch the Torah with his *tallit*, his prayer shawl, and sing the Hebrew blessing he's been practicing for months. Later, I am told that when his voice rang out over the congregation, raspy and proud, people cried.

He doesn't want to go to my house and rest after the service. He doesn't want to miss the celebration. He doesn't leave early—he stays and smiles for four hours of eating and dancing.

Two months after the bar mitzvah ceremony, his kidneys fail.

There is another family meeting on the subject of the nursing home. This one takes place outside, on my parents' deck. The rabbi has been asked to be present as a kind of arbitrator in this unbearable discussion. We hope we will behave more rationally, less emotionally, in front of an outsider. This time, my mother is present.

It's a Sunday afternoon on a mild day in April. My mother is serving tea and cookies, and as the rabbi selects one, he tells her how much he enjoys this custom. The rabbi was born in Hungary, and there is something formal and old-world about sitting down to afternoon tea. We are careful to be polite and civilized as the teapot makes its rounds.

Beneath the veneer of courtesy, I am nervous and edgy. There is nothing truly convivial about this occasion. We are here to try to convince my father to go into a nursing home.

Since December, when he went into kidney failure, he spends nine hours a week—three three-hour sessions—hooked up to a dialysis machine at the local dialysis center. Dialysis exhausts him, and he sleeps most of the time he's not hooked up.

The events leading to the diagnosis of renal failure were terrifying—one day my mother discovered him in bed, having a seizure. Although my mother has hired a car service to help with the driving to the dialysis center, she often has to drive when the roads are icy or covered with snow. My father's decline makes her feel even more helpless and responsible.

I cannot remember what was said at this meeting, although I remember that Larry and I did most of the talking. Although I don't recall our exact words, I can still hear our voices reaching a kind of crescendo before they subsided.

We tried to state clearly that we didn't want to send my father to a nursing home. We tried to emphasize that such a step had become necessary because of the increasing demands of his illness and the stress it inflicted on our mother.

We explained, complained, pleaded, cajoled, threatened, temporized, and, finally, apologized.

My father insisted that he did not want to give up his home, although he did say he would try to be more open-minded about my mother's predicament as his caregiver.

When the meeting is over, the rabbi walks me to the front door and clasps my hand. He tells me that Larry and I are doing a good job in a difficult situation, and that not all children would stand by their parents this way. I feel my eyes well up in gratitude that someone has acknowledged the impossibility of our position. I am grateful that he does not see me as some kind of monster who wants to send her father away.

I decide I am never going to another family meeting.

There was one more family meeting.

After four years of full-time caregiving, my mother decides to take a vacation. She signs up for a five-day trip to Santa Fe sponsored by a local art museum. I can't see why she wants to travel to the other side of the country; I think she should take a less ambitious journey and stay closer to home. I guess I'm nervous about being in charge in her absence.

Her departure raises the question of what to do about my father. Because the aide does not drive, my mother is worried about leaving my father at home. His blood pressure and blood sugar are very unstable; my mother thinks he would not get proper medical attention. So she arranges for him to spend a week in a nursing home called Northridge Manor, through what is called respite care.

When my mother returns from her trip, she decides she can no longer endure the responsibility of my father's illness. The weekday aide who took care of my father for nearly four years has just given notice, and the ongoing situation of having a different aide each weekend has been a disaster.

The strain has become unendurable for her, for us. She wants my father to stay at the nursing home as a full-time patient.

My father is enraged. He agreed to a week's visit, not a permanent stay. He wants to go home.

It is against the law for someone to be kept in a nursing home against his or her will. My father demands a meeting with the nursing home administration.

The meeting takes place in the Northridge Manor conference room, at a large oval-shaped table. My father is seated in his wheelchair at one end of the table; opposite him is the director of the nursing home. The rest of us take our seats. In addition to my mother, my brother, and me, there is the rabbi, my aunt, a new elder-care case manager and her assistant, two physical therapists from the nursing home staff, and the director of nursing. I realize this is the largest meeting my father has been to since his illness.

The director of the nursing home runs the meeting.

This is proper, because this is her turf. I am relieved; I was afraid it would be a free-for-all, with my family hurling accusations, curses, and blame at one another. Nonetheless, underneath the table I am wringing my hands.

We proceed at a civilized pace. The director asks my father if he has been pleased with the level of care he has received, whether he has found the staff attentive, whether he has judged the physical therapy helpful. The meals here: have they been to his liking? My father is diffident, noncommittal, dismissive. These questions don't interest him.

Then she gets to the good stuff: "Charles, would you like to continue to stay with us?" And my father exclaims, in a voice rough and gravelly, "No!"

Silence. No one says a word.

I look at the table as though it were a Ouija board. The air is thick with tension.

Then the director asks my mother if she would like to speak. My mother, to my great surprise, given the amount of stress she is under, speaks eloquently, articulately. She describes the difficulties of being a full-time caregiver: the loneliness, the exhaustion, the overwhelming responsibility. "I feel totally alone," she says. "People in agencies move on; friends and family have lives of their own. There's no one I can turn to." She says that as my father's health has deteriorated, she worries more and more that she cannot give him the care he needs. She feels she is required to make medical decisions she's not qualified to make. She knows that here, he would receive proper attention.

The director turns to my father. "Your wife has made some very good points, Charles. I agree with her that we are better equipped to take of you. We have round-the-clock nursing staff, which you don't have at home. Isn't that important to you?"

"No."

"And your wife? Her own health is being compromised as a result of the demands of your care. Don't you care about that?"

"No."

There are gasps from a few of the women at the table. They seem appalled. I want to apologize for my father's selfishness, to tell the staff they must understand he is a drowning man. Everyone knows that those who are drowning will inadvertently try to submerge the very people who are trying to save them.

Silence.

Maybe the meeting is over? What more is there to be said?

Before I know what I am doing, I am on my feet, shouting. Something has erupted inside me, all the molten pain and fury I've felt these past few years. I hear myself shrieking in a voice I don't recognize.

"I can't stand this anymore! I can't stand watching my parents struggle with illness and with each other. I can't stand being caught in the middle, trying to help one parent at the expense of the other. I cannot be asked to make decisions I have no authority to carry out. I am being torn apart. From here on out, I will not participate in any more meetings! I am through, finished with all of this! I'm done!"

I was not eloquent, not articulate. I don't even know if those were my words. When I finish speaking, the meeting breaks up.

I approach my father to try to talk with him, but he will not look at me. As my aunt wheels my father toward his room, I hear him ask whether he can live with her.

My mother comes over to me and puts her arm around me. She says she is sorry; she had no idea I was so upset. The people from the nursing home pass by me in a blur. I tell her I'm sorry I lost my temper. She hugs me. Then I drive home.

Two days after this meeting, my father comes home.

In May of 2000, I graduate from Rutgers with a doctorate in English. My father cannot attend the ceremony. There are hundreds of graduates sitting on folding chairs on the floor of the indoor stadium, thousands of friends and family in the bleachers. Robert Pinsky, the Poet Laureate, gives the commencement address.

It has taken me twelve years to get my Ph.D. My father has told me that finishing my degree is one of three things he wants to see before he dies. The first was Josh's *bar mitzvah* ceremony, the second my brother's marriage. My brother has no plans to get married, so two out of three isn't bad.

One month after my graduation, we are told my father's leg has to come off. Above the knee.

My father has lost his battle against diabetes. For months now, the sores on his feet have refused to heal. One day the podiatrist gives him the terrible news: he has gangrene.

I thought gangrene died with the soldiers of World War I. It's antediluvian, anachronistic. People don't die of blood poisoning anymore—after all, this is the beginning of the new millennium. But new millennium or not, he is going to lose his left leg. The paralysis of this limb has exacerbated the circulation problems associated with diabetes.

My father does not want to have his leg amputated. He says he would rather die of the infection. "Let me die already," he says to us.

The doctor tells him that gangrene is a gruesome death. It is slow and excruciatingly painful, even with morphine to dull the stabbing. It can take months to die of gangrene. "The body putrefies," the nurses whisper to my mother. "The stench is awful."

All right, so dying of gangrene is not an option. The amputation is scheduled.

My father's leg is amputated on July 20, 2000, my forty-fourth birthday. On the way to the hospital the day of the surgery my car is rear-ended at a busy entrance to Route 46. I get out and start yelling at the shaken young woman who drove the car that hit me. "My father is having his leg amputated today," I want to scream.

At the hospital, my father is in great pain—he moans and thrashes his head and shoulders. He cannot take any painkillers before the operation.

The minutes tick slowly by as my mother and I wait for the attendants to get him. As soon as they place him on the gurney, I rush out of the room, get in my car, and race for home.

After the amputation I have nightmares about the missing leg.

"What happens to amputated limbs?" I ask my husband. He says they are disposed of with the medical waste.

The thought of my father's leg being dumped in the garbage is too much to bear. I have visions of finding it and bringing it back to life. When I go to the hospital to visit him after the surgery, I cannot rid myself of the idea that the leg is inside a closet, waiting for me to resuscitate it.

My father stops speaking. He will answer a question with a monosyllable, but that's about it. I recently found a letter dated July 23, 2000, that I wrote but never sent:

Dear Dad,

I am writing to you because every time I see you I am filled with emotion and find it hard to express my feelings. We are all very sorry for the terrible thing that has befallen you. We know that you are suffering. None of us will ever know how much.

That said, we also suffer. The world isn't black and white. Although we can't feel your pain, that doesn't mean we feel no pain.

We cannot bring back to you what you have lost, but we still have something to give you—our deep, abiding love. You are still the head of our family. I am begging you to try to come to terms with this loss. We are here for you; please don't turn us away.

Your loving daughter,
Nancy

I don't regret not sending this letter. What difference would it have made?

I wish I had sent the letter.

Two months after the amputation, my father goes into Northridge Manor as a full-time resident. The new aide can't get him out of bed. He does not have the strength to help with transfers from the bed to the wheelchair. It takes two very strong people to lift him.

This time, there are no arguments, no family meetings. We have run out of options.

Northridge Manor looks something like a hotel. The halls are papered in a cheerful red-and-white chrysanthemum pattern, with deep green carpeting to match. If you close your eyes to the people in wheelchairs and the nurses at their stations, you might pretend you are in a Hilton. There is even a tiny coffee shop with a few scattered bistro tables and chairs.

My father likes to be taken to the coffee shop for ice cream floats, which are made with sugar-free ice cream and Diet Coke for diabetic patients like him. He can make that drink last for a good half hour. These outings for ice cream make our visits easier for me, because they give us something to do.

When I visit the nursing home, I arrive buoyed by a sense of mission and purpose: I am here to do a *mitzvah*, a good deed: to spend time with my sick father. I am cheered by the silk flowers on the lobby table and the announcement of the week's activities on the bulletin board. "This isn't such a bad place," I console myself.

But by the time I reach his floor, I am shaken. There is no use pretending that this is some kind of vacation spot—reminders are everywhere that this is the final destination. In the dayroom men and women doze in their metal chairs. From one of the rooms a woman's voice keeps crying, "Nurse, Nurse!" Beneath the sickly sweet smell of antiseptic wafts another odor—familiar, unpleasant, soiled.

My father's room is at the end of a long corridor. Usually he is sleeping when I arrive. A private-duty aide hired by my mother sits in a chair, reading or watching television.

Sometimes he opens his eyes and says, "Hi, *schaetzle.*" Sometimes he doesn't respond to my greeting until the aide nudges his shoulder and says, "Charlie, Charlie. Nancy is here."

During these visits I try to assume an air of bravado, thinking maybe I can cheer or distract him. We don't have much to talk about. Any subject I can think of—my children, sports, current events, even the weather—especially the weather, since he rarely goes outside—only deepens the chasm between us. I am part of the living world, and my father is not.

I also suspect he is angry with me because he thinks I have betrayed him: I participated in the family conspiracy that put him in here.

One Sunday afternoon, I wheel my father down the hall of Northridge Manor toward the elevator that will take us to the coffee shop on the first floor.

As we wait, a patient in a print housedress creeps toward us, leaning on her walker. I estimate that she is a good ten years older than my father, because the majority of residents here are in their eighties. When she reaches us she stops and looks my father up and down as if appraising a valuable bronze vase.

"He's a very nice-looking man," she says to me. Then she moves on down the hall.

"Well, Dad," I say, making an attempt at humor. "I guess you can still charm the ladies." He grunts in reply.

Having failed to make my father laugh, I try my brother. He points out that the ratio of women to men at Northridge Manor is two to one. "If you're still breathing, they think you're a good catch," he says.

Three years before the stroke, as a surprise gift for my father's seventieth birthday, my brother and I had created a kind of "this is your life" photo scrapbook. We bought a handsome leather album and sent out a call for pictures among family and the German contingent of my father's friends. When my father was out of the house, my mother searched my father's bureau, where old photos were scattered among tie clips, cuff links, ancient keys, foreign coins, socks, and handkerchiefs. My brother and I arranged to meet at my house to edit and organize the photos, which Larry took home and assembled, using his keen photographer's eye, into aesthetically pleasing pages.

It took us several hours to sort through hundreds of photos, which we laid out on my kitchen table. We started with the earliest ones, pictures of my father's childhood in Germany. Images of my father as a baby. Riding a bicycle with his father. A rare image of him with his mother, father, and sister.

We organized the album chronologically. There was a page devoted to his days as a soccer player for the New World Club. A page with photos of various ski buddies on trips to the Catskills. Photos of my parents' wedding, all the way up through photos of him holding his grandchildren.

There were so many pictures of him with former girlfriends that we decided to do a page entitled "The Swinging Bachelor." People said this might offend my mother, but she laughed when we told her our plan. She knew my father had gone out with many women from his social set before he proposed to her. "That happened a long time ago," she said.

I feel guilty all the time.

The women of the support group and I agreed that we always felt guilty. Guilty that we weren't always available for our parents. Guilty that we wanted our own lives. Guilty that we sometimes felt angry with them. Guilty that we couldn't change things.

The group facilitator used to ask us, "Do you think this guilt is productive? Does it help you become better caregivers?"

We knew the answer to these questions was "no," but the fact was we felt guilty anyway.

My father is sitting in his wheelchair. He is dressed in chinos and an undershirt. His shirt is lying crumpled on the bed because it is so hot in the room. This gives me a perfect opportunity to have him try on the

Hanukkah presents I have brought with me. One is a wool cardigan, which I immediately realize is much too warm for this place; the other is a silk and cotton pullover.

I want to help him put on the pullover, but I'm afraid of his withered left arm. "How do I do this, Dad? Do I pull it over your head first?"

"No, first you pull my left arm through the sleeve," he says. This makes no sense; surely this must be wrong. I bunch up the shirt, pulling it slowly across the shrunken arm, then down over the head, then over the right arm. It wasn't as difficult as I'd imagined. The silky cotton rests comfortably on his skin. I stroke the sleeve. "It looks nice on you, Dad. It's a good color for you." My father studies the shirt. "It's gray, isn't it?" he asks.

When I leave, my father reminds me that I have promised to exchange the wool sweater for something lighter and more comfortable. I am happy; I have accomplished something. This visit, at least, has been a success.

The smell of the nursing home is something else. There is an odor of disinfectant masking the smell of human waste. I try not to breathe through my nose when I visit, which means that by the time I leave, I have a terrible headache.

The halls are scrupulously clean, so it's not that the place looks dirty. No, the soiling is elsewhere, and not just inside the utility closets. It's wrapped around the heart, hidden among the tangled sheets. It's written on faces, bodies like mashed fruit. Women with red and purple bruises on their arms and legs, the scars of diabetes. Women with hair as fine as gossamer silk and smiles as sad as a goodnight kiss. Men babbling or groaning. Men in the halls thrusting their shriveled arms in my face. "Won't you fix my footrest, miss? Please, won't you help me?"

I try not to look or listen. I walk down these corridors rapidly, my eyes focused forward, my thoughts focused inward. I must minimize what I see. I have my own sorrows to contend with. I cannot help these people.

I am on my way out of Northridge Manor after one of my silent visits with my father. As I approach the lobby, I see a man in a wheelchair, a one-legged man like my father, trying to push his chair over an area rug toward the door that leads to the outside world. Unlike my father, he can use both arms to move his chair. But the carpet has buckled in the corner, and he cannot get the momentum he needs to carry him across.

I stand a few feet behind him so he can't see me watching. He rolls the wheels backward, so that the chair goes in reverse, then pushes them forward rapidly. No luck. He repeats the process, to no avail.

I am torn between wanting to help him and rushing out the door to freedom. This man is not my problem, I think. Where are the aides, anyhow? Why is it that I seem to be the only one aware of his difficulty? Is it my job to assist him when I can do nothing for my father?

Before I can answer these questions, I find myself approaching him and asking if he would like some help. He gratefully accepts. I wheel him through the door, where two patients—a man and a woman, who look to be in their sixties—are sitting in wheelchairs next to the concrete columns that support a kind of portico to protect visitors from bad weather. Today, the weather is mild and sunny, and my throat clenches as I realize I should have brought my father outside. Even though my father usually says no if you ask him if he wants to go outside.

There is not enough room to put this man's chair next to his friends, so I place him a few feet away, just far enough away that he is unable to reach the cigarette the woman offers him. He asks me if I will hand it to him. What are you, crazy? I want to scream. Isn't it enough that I took you out here and now you want one of those cancer sticks to boot? Isn't it bad enough that you've already lost one leg? What do you want, to lose the other one? But I don't know this man, and I don't say these things. I hand him the cigarette.

Then he asks me if I'll light a match for him. I've had just about enough of this, I want to say. I'm tired, I had a bad visit with my father, this place makes me sick, I want to go home. But I light the match for him and walk quickly away before he can ask anything else.

As I get in my car, I realize that if I were stuck in a nursing home with one leg and wanted to smoke a cigarette outside, I'd damn well do it.

My father is lying on a mattress on the floor of Northridge Manor. He has been on the floor for several weeks, ever since he tried to climb out of bed. With only one leg, this was an effort that was doomed to failure.

When I asked him why he did it, he said he didn't know. I believe him. The stroke damaged his frontal lobe, known as the executive center of the brain, which controls judgment and critical thinking. He doesn't know why he tried to climb out of bed. Maybe he thought he could walk again. Maybe he wanted to run away.

The staff at the nursing home is convinced he was trying to commit suicide. When I ask him if this is true, he laughs bitterly and says no. I believe him.

The episode of the mattress was precipitated by an earlier event, when my father slipped out of his wheelchair and hit his head on the metal rails of his bed. After a great deal of urging from the staff, he agreed to go to the hospital, where tests revealed he was suffering from a hematoma. The day before he was scheduled to be discharged from the hospital, back to the nursing home, I spoke to him on the phone. He was very agitated and wanted to know why he couldn't go home, to the house where my mother lives, where he had lived for forty-five years.

"I am so sorry, Dad. I don't know what to say."

"You're in cahoots with your mother," he said. "It's a conspiracy. You put me in a nursing home."

"No, Dad. I didn't put you in a nursing home. Mom didn't put you in a nursing home. The stroke put you in a nursing home."

I don't know where clarity came from. I don't know how I found those words. I only knew I was getting tired of that place of guilt. I had been in that place for years now, and I wanted out. I had been working hard in therapy to find a way out. Once you peek over the edge of the abyss of self-recrimination, there's another landscape, a new vista of freedom. I wanted to be in that picture, in that guilt-free place. Besides, what I said to him was the honest truth.

"Besides, it's too expensive for you to stay at home," I continued. Bingo. Big mistake.

My father picked right up on it. "See? I knew it," he said. "I knew it was really about money." I could hear the anger in his voice; I could hear myself sighing, regretting my words.

"No, it isn't a question of money at all. It is expensive to take care of you at home, but that's not the reason you're not there. Mom can't do it anymore. Your care is very difficult. It takes two aides to lift you. Half the time the aides don't show up. How many aides have worked with you since you became ill? I've lost track, and so have you. Your care is too much to manage. You can't expect Mom to run a nursing home. She's done it all these years, and she can't do it anymore. It's not that she doesn't want to. She just can't."

Silence. A thundering silence. After a few moments my father grunted. I knew he heard me; I knew I had reached him. "Nobody wants this, Dad. This is what happened because of the stroke."

After a few angry letters and phone calls from my brother, my father goes back into a bed.

One Sunday, while we are sitting together in silence, a woman wearing a beige suit and a silk blouse enters and introduces herself as Dr. Sandra Lang, the nursing home psychologist. She opens my father's chart and takes out a pen. My father has been a patient here for several months, and to my knowledge, this is the first time he has met Dr. Lang. On the other hand, he is no longer interested in talking to psychologists and psychiatrists. From his perspective, they've done nothing to help him.

"Let's see what we have here," Dr. Lang says brightly. "It says that you've been telling the nurses you don't want to be here. Is that true?"

"Yes."

I can feel my stomach winding itself into knots. What the hell is she doing, stirring this stuff up, I think. We've been over this ground for years. Who the hell is she to come in here and start with this now?

"Where would you go if you left Northridge?" she asks.

"I'd go home," he says.

"You have a home to go to?" she asks. She turns to me. "If he has a home, why isn't he there?"

I can feel my blood pressure soaring, my face turning red. I turn to the aide for support, but she looks straight ahead and says nothing. "My mother can't take care of him at home." I'm not sure if my words are audible or not. It takes all my energy to stay seated and not get up and punch her.

Dr. Lang puts her hand on my father's shoulder. "Is that true?" she asks. "Is it true your wife can't take care of you at home?"

"Yes," my father says.

"Why not?" she asks.

"I'm too sick," he says. "I have one leg."

Dr. Lang is busy writing in her chart. "Are you on antidepressants?" she asks my father.

"No."

"Why not?"

"I don't know."

It's been years since I kept track of my father's medications. At one time I knew exactly what he was taking. I remember that his psychiatrist prescribed Wellbutrin a long time ago. I also know that when my father was angry with my mother, or the aide, or his life, he refused to take the antidepressant. He knew exactly which little pill it was and would not open his mouth for it. I imagine he's taking something now, but I have to admit I'm not sure. I suddenly feel terribly inadequate.

Dr. Lang turns to me. "Your father is very depressed, you know," she says. "You should make sure he is taking an antidepressant."

Fuck you, I think.

Dr. Lang closes the chart. "Well, Charles, I enjoyed meeting you. I hope you start feeling better."

"Thank you."

Dr. Sandra Lang touches my father's shoulder again and leaves.

For a few minutes I sit glued to my chair, my skin tingling in anger. How dare a stranger come in and speak like this? How dare she stir things up without knowing the story of what has come before?

Shortly after Dr. Lang leaves, I decide to end my visit and look for her. I find her at the nurses' station, writing on a pad. "Dr. Lang," I say, "I know that you are just trying to do your job, but my father has a very long history of illness. It has been very difficult for us to convince him to come here, and you know nothing about it. And he's wrong about having a home to go to," I add. "There is no home for him anymore." I hope I never see Dr. Lang again, and I don't care what she thinks of me.

Dr. Lang regards me with a detached smile. "It's my job to make sure that patients want to be here. It's against the law for a patient to stay here against their will. Your father seems very unhappy to me."

I shake my head in disbelief. Happiness is hardly the point, I want to say. Do the other residents seem happy to you? But I don't say this. I don't have the energy to argue anymore. "My father has a long history that you know nothing about. You know nothing about him or our family," I repeat. I leave, feeling once again I have failed.

My anger doesn't seem to matter, because that's the last we see of Dr. Sandra Lang.

My father's silences are wearing me out. I decide to try visiting him in the morning. On Sundays I usually arrive around 3:00 in the afternoon, which can be a low point even for those of us who are healthy. One morning I decide to surprise him and visit while the kids are at school.

When I get to his room at 10:30, it is empty. Alarmed that something might be wrong, I approach one of the nurses, who tells me he has gone to recreational therapy, on the first floor. She tells me I'm welcome to look in on him.

The recreational therapist, a lively woman in her mid-fifties named Becky, is standing inside a circle ringed by patients. She and I are the only people who are not in wheelchairs.

There are twelve patients, ten of whom are women. People are in varying states of awareness, with my father among the most lucid. Some seem to be dozing; others are awake but do not seem to connect to their surroundings.

Becky is playing a game; standing in the center of the circle, she tosses an inflated beach ball at each of the patients, who have to hold out their arms to catch it. I look at my father, who is eagerly awaiting his turn. When the ball appears in front of him, he reaches out with his one good arm and maneuvers it onto his lap. I haven't seen him this engaged for a long time. I don't know whether to laugh or to cry.

Next comes a game of ring toss, and the session is almost over. "Now it's time for 'YMCA,'" announces Becky. People clap. Becky turns to me. "Your father loves this," she says as she turns on the boom box. And there they are, filling the corners of the room: the voices of the Village People.

"Y—M—C—A, it's fun to go to the Y—M—C—A," the patients chant. Even the somnolent ones are awake now. They are all doing the hand motions from their wheelchairs, including my father, who uses his one good arm. Well, what the hell? I join in, with my arms over my head. "Y—M—C—A, it's fun to go to the Y—M—C—A." The patients are singing and laughing, and I laugh, too, while tears slide down my face. I can't remember the last time I saw my father having a good time.

I don't blame anyone for what happened to my father; I blame the stroke. I used to blame everyone: my mother, for not suffering silently; my father, for suffering silently; my brother, for not understanding that I was sandwiched between my parents and my children; Dr. Fox, for not warning my father that he was at risk; the professionals, for their suggestions that never seemed to help; the physical therapists, for their optimism; the poets, for not giving me words for my grief; God, for punishing him.

"Blaspheme God, and die," says Job's wife to her husband, the only words she pronounces among the thousands that make up her husband's book.

God says to the Adversary (*ha-satan,* in Hebrew), "Behold my servant Job. He is a blameless, upright man who fears God and shuns evil." And the Adversary replies, "Does Job not have a reason to fear God? You have blessed him so that his possessions spread out in the land. But lay Your hand upon all that he has, and he will surely blaspheme You to Your face."

So God tests Job. His children are killed in a storm. His livestock perish in a fire. He is covered with boils and festering sores. But still he will not denounce God, although he complains bitterly and asks for an end to his suffering.

My father has been a resident of Northridge Manor for about nine months when suddenly he becomes very ill. Out of the blue, he spikes a fever of 103; he is delirious and is sent to the hospital. The doctors determine that the fever is caused by a staph infection; after a few days of testing, they discover he has a strain of staphylococcus that cannot be treated with antibiotics and is incurable.

We speak with Arnie, my brother's friend, who specializes in infectious diseases. He says it is not uncommon for dialysis patients to develop such infections, and that this particular strain is always fatal.

After consulting with the doctors, my father is taken off anything that would sustain life: food, water, insulin, all medications. Even so, he lingers.

There is nothing worse than watching a loved one die. At the end, after all the years of planning, coping, and managing, things fall apart once again. We do not make visitation schedules. Sometimes the three of us are there in my father's room, sometimes one of us is there— sometimes, no one is there. The hours and days creep by.

There is nothing we can do but watch. At first he is restless and moans, but then he is too weak to do anything. A nurse comes in periodically and adjusts the level of morphine in his IV. Or she gives us washcloths and cups of chipped ice so we can wipe his lips, which are dry and cracked. He is not unconscious, but he is too exhausted to speak. It is not a beautiful death.

How did we get the idea that death should be beautiful? Maybe from nineteenth-century sentimental novels, where the family gathers around the deathbed of the loved one, who is gazing beatifically toward the heavens and saying things like, "I'm ready now."

Take the story of Beth, for instance, the third of the March sisters in *Little Women*. After a long, debilitating illness, during which she somehow manages to read and sing, Beth finally draws her last breath. She is peaceful, serene, and Marmee and the three sisters are comforted that she has greeted death as "a benignant angel, not a phantom full of dread." In death as in life, Beth has taken care of her family's needs before her own—she has been the perfect daughter.

The days somehow pass. Word has spread that my father is dying, and people come to pay their respects. A few hold his hand as they whisper good-bye. My father doesn't open his eyes. I don't remember whether he muttered anything or not.

The blackboard on the wall in his hospital room is filled with phrases like "If I knew the way, I would take you home" and "One way or another, this darkness got to give"—written by my brother, who borrowed them from songs by the Grateful Dead.

One of my father's tennis buddies, a rabbi who had supervised the synagogue religious school when I was a student there, comes to say farewell. "It's time, Charlie," he says, taking my father's hand. "You can let go now." I hold my breath. "Oh my God," I think. "This is it. It's going to happen, and I'm going to be the only one here from my family." But nothing happens.

The doctors tell us that if he hangs on for more than a week, he will be transferred back to the nursing home. I pray he won't.

On the day that turns out to be his last, I find myself at the hospital at about 6:00 in the evening. My brother and mother have been there since early morning. I tell them to go home and rest, then I take a seat next to his bed.

About 7:00, Sarah, a friend of my parents, comes in. When visitors arrive, I move away from the bed and sit a few feet away, against the wall, in order to give the newcomers a chance to talk to my father. Sarah takes my father's hand and says hello. She asks my father if he knows who is there. To my astonishment, my father opens his eyes and says her name. She bends down and murmurs some words in his ear. This, too, is a surprise; most people maintain a distance from my father, fearing they might catch his infection, even though it is not contagious. Then she leaves.

I am filled with envy. I've been on a death watch for five days, and my father has not acknowledged me. I want him to say my name.

I pull my chair over to his bed and lift his hand, which is thin and translucent as an onion skin. "Dad," I say. "Do you know who this is?"

Silence.

"Dad," I press on. "Say my name."

Silence. I am in turmoil, angry at myself for making demands of a dying man, angry at him for what feels like stubbornness.

"Dad, I know you're in there."

Silence. I am about to give up when, out of the blue, I hear, "Nancy."

I am overjoyed that he has made contact. I move even closer and bend my head to meet his. I want desperately to maintain the connection. I can think of nothing meaningful at this moment, so I say, "This isn't easy, is it?" And my father whispers, "Nothing is easy."

And then, silence. I know that this silence will be the longest one, that my father will not speak to me again.

And indeed, those are the last words he says to me. That evening, shortly after midnight, my father slips into a coma and passes away. We are not there to send him off. He dies alone.

When I think back to that evening, I try to recall if I knew it would be his last. I try to remember whether the night nurse, who watched me leave at 9:00 P.M., raised her eyebrows, as if to ask me where did I think I was going. These are the traces of guilt playing tricks with my imagination. The nurses see all kinds of families and all kinds of deaths. Throughout my father's days, they were efficient and professional. They tried to relieve my father's suffering, but they did not offer advice or sympathy, which was a great relief. If they judge the actions of the living, they have the decency to keep their opinions to themselves.

There was no deathbed scene, no family gathering, no hand-holding, no chanting of prayers or hymns. When I tell this to an acquaintance, she is horrified. She tells me the story of how her family helped her father leave this world for the next. They kept vigil for hours, she says, for days, even. When I talk about how unbearable it was at the end, how, ultimately, none of us could stand to watch the suffering anymore, another friend says she still feels guilty that she wasn't with her mother when her mother passed away.

There is no proper way to die, and there are no rules. We must all live with our own consciences; we have no authority to declare to our fellow travelers, "You should have done this, or done that."

> And you, my father, there on the sad height,
> Curse, bless, me now with fierce tears, I pray.
> Do not go gentle into that good night.
> Rage, rage, against the dying of the light.

My father died in the early morning hours of Tuesday, June 19, 2001. He was buried the next day. According to Jewish law, burial should take place as quickly as possible, although not during the Sabbath. Custom dictates that the deceased be buried in a plain pine coffin (always closed during the service) and mourned for seven days.

For years Jews have fiddled with these traditions. My father was buried in a walnut coffin—a little more elegant—and my mother sat *shivah* for three days. There are other rules governing cremation, which is forbidden in Jewish law, and the donation of organs for research or transplantation, verboten as well. I know Jewish families who have ignored these prohibitions. But I have never seen an open coffin at a Jewish funeral.

On Monday afternoon, June 17, my brother and I meet with the rabbi at my mother's house. My mother and Larry had chosen the coffin shortly after we heard that my father's infection could not be treated. The funeral home had been alerted. Phone calls to friends and family were being made. All that remained, for now, was the order of the service. Did Larry and I want to speak? the rabbi asked. Yes, we did. The rabbi said that Larry would speak first, then me, then anyone else who felt moved to do so.

On my way home from the meeting, I stop at Talbots, the women's clothing store. Early that morning I had opened my closet to see what, if anything, I owned that I could wear to a funeral. All I saw were three pairs of baggy black linen pants. I decided to have a little talk with myself:

> *Voice 1*: You're not going to wear those old wrinkled things, are you?
> *Voice 2*: It's a funeral, not a fashion show. No one cares what I wear. They're black, and they fit.
> *Voice 1*: What's wrong with you? Don't you have any pride in your appearance?
> *Voice 2*: As a matter of fact, I do. I'll stop at Talbots on the way home and see if I can find anything.
> *Voice 1*: Thatta girl! Your father would be proud of you.
> *Voice 2*: I'm not doing this for my father. I'm doing it for me.
> *Voice 1*: You know, I think you may be growing up.

At Talbots I wander around in a daze. A saleswoman approached and asks if I need help. "I need a dark outfit for a funeral," I say. "My father's funeral," I add. The expression of concern on her face rearranges itself into alarm—am I going to start sobbing?—but I am too numb and exhausted for that. I want a suit, not sympathy.

The saleswoman rose to the occasion and finds me a pearl-gray silk suit—a long skirt with a matching jacket. Miraculously, both fit, although the skirt touches my ankles and the jacket sleeves graze my fingertips. "Take it to the woman at the tailor's next door," the saleswoman urges. "Tell her it's an emergency."

I don't need any urging. I march next door and hand the woman my suit. "Could you please have this for me tomorrow?" I say. "I need it for my father's funeral." The woman nods and takes it from me without a word.

I think the chapel at the funeral home was full. It seemed as though a few hundred people filled the pews. The rabbi had told me that he would lead a brief service, and then ask us to speak.

I sat in the front pew and stared straight ahead, trying hard not to lose my composure. The rabbi must have noticed my effort, because he changed the order of speakers and asked me to speak first, before my brother. I was grateful for his sensitivity, because I was rapidly losing my grip.

Giving a eulogy in front of that crowd of people was one of the most difficult trials I've ever faced. I had prepared a brief text, in which I tried to capture my father's spirit:

"As you know, my father was a CPA, an accountant. But his personality did not go with the job description. He was far more interested in people than in debits and credits. He had a wonderful sense of humor, and even when he was very ill he could still make people laugh. I know that he would be pleased that so many dear friends and family have come today to honor him.

"Friendship mattered a great deal to him. Some of his friendships went back over fifty years, to his early days as an immigrant to this country. He made friends from many avenues and interests: UJA, B'nai B'rith, the synagogue, tennis, bridge, work. When my father liked you, he liked you for life.

"My father was a tenacious man. If you'd ever played tennis with him, you'd know what I mean. He chased down every ball as though his life depended on it. Out of respect for his memory, I will say nothing about his line calls.

"My father's last words were, 'Nothing is easy.' I think they testify to his fighting spirit, his tenacity. I think he was trying to tell me that a life well lived requires hard work. He worked hard all his life, and most especially when he was ill. He has earned this final rest."

I rested my hand on the luminous wood of the coffin as I left the podium to return to my seat. It flashed through my mind that the gesture might appear theatrical, but I didn't care. This was my final chance to say good-bye.

My brother talked about Aaron Copeland's "Fanfare for the Common Man" and how it reminded him of my father: heroic, triumphant, accessible.

My mother read a selection from Ecclesiastes, known to the children of the sixties as a protest song by The Byrds: "To Everything Turn, Turn, Turn."

After that, memory blurs. Several other people spoke, and most of them mentioned my father's infamous line calls, where the opponent's ball was always out. I'm not sure whether he would have found that funny.

Three years have passed since my father died, and I still ruminate on the stroke and whether his suffering and ours could have been prevented.

In my search for answers, I went looking through my father's business diaries, which my mother showed me one day. My father was not much of a correspondent, so I have no letters from him. I had not known he'd kept a diary of sorts, so the stash of volumes satisfied both my need to have something he'd written and my desire to learn how much he understood about his health and the risks at stake.

I was wrong to imagine he'd known he was in grave danger. In the diary for 1995 I found a letter, dated April 3, 1995, from Dr. Fox at the hypertension clinic, five months before the stroke:

Dear Mr. Frankel,
   The results of the chemistry screenings tests are generally excellent, demonstrating normal kidney and liver function. Blood sugar was 93; it was 298 in July 1994. Protein bound glucose is only mildly elevated—1.4—demonstrating generally good control of the diabetes. Total cholesterol is 269—it was 251 in July 1994. HDL (good) cholesterol is 42; a level over 45 is associated with lower risk of coronary artery disease. Your blood pressure was under good control—156/85. Please continue the medications at their present level.
   Best wishes for a healthy spring.

                                                   Sincerely,
                                                   Dr. Louis Fox

As far as I can tell, the only red flag in this report is high cholesterol, and I'm not sure my father understood cholesterol was a major threat. In any case, there are no explicit warnings from Dr. Fox.

The diaries record the rich, full life of a busy man. They are handsome books, chestnut-colored leather with an alligator pattern. He received them as yearly Christmas gifts from a company from which he purchased insurance against credit card fraud. I guess such insurance was inexpensive and worth the peace of mind. I tried to contact the company and order one for myself, but a Google search told me the top executives had been indicted for fraud, and the firm had gone under.

Tucked inside the diary for 1995—his last one—along with the letter from Dr. Fox, were all kinds of papers: receipts for plumbing and heating maintenance; business cards from electricians and repair contractors; strips of paper with names and phone numbers of bridge and tennis partners; concert programs; a brochure for East Hampton House, where he and my mother spent a long weekend a month before the stroke.

At the top of each page of the diary is a quote, which I suspect did not interest my father a great deal. There's an interesting range of voices, from Robert Kennedy—"Only those who fail greatly can ever achieve greatly"—to Bernard Baruch—"Vote for the man who promises least; he'll be the least disappointing"—to Lord Byron—"The great art of life is sensation, to feel that we exist, even in pain." How true, Lord Byron, how true.

Each day contains a few mere jottings. Here's a typical entry: "Odds and ends. Finished McAllister payroll taxes. Unity Concerts." Or, "Lunch with Ely and the boys at diner. Movies with Trudy; saw 'Nobody's Fool.'" Or, on a Sunday: "Larry here; watched Browns v. New England."

He also documented the weather: "Hot and humid." "Beautiful day, 70 degrees." The entry for Friday, February 24, 1995: "Cool today. Great bridge. Nancy attacked."

I was attacked, mugged by an unknown assailant who sneaked up on me behind my back, hit me on the head with his ringed fist, and ran off with my purse while I was trying to unlock my kitchen door. I had forgotten the date. It's curious to me that my father noted it in the same detached tone he used to record watching a football game. On the other hand, in the shock of reading those words, "Nancy attacked," I think I hear the echoes of his own distress.

Caregiving is a solo flight through unmarked territory. There are no maps, no guides. You must find your way alone.

Ruth Ray defines caregiving as an activity that involves intimacy and connection, in which care is given freely. Yes, I was a caregiver.

Sometimes I ask myself what I learned from my father's illness.

I've learned to slow down a bit. I've learned to be less afraid of speaking my mind. I've learned about my own ageism, the fear and distrust of age rampant in a culture that denies it. I'm still learning.

What did my father learn, if anything, from his illness?

That is a more complicated question. He never spoke to me directly about how his understanding of himself changed. He had moved quite suddenly from a place of privilege and dominance within our family to one of powerlessness and invisibility. Even though my life revolved around the stroke for six years, the demands of his illness drove my actions and emotions, rather than my dealings with him and the new person he had become.

I regret that I was not able to get to know my new father. Whenever I saw him, I wanted the old one back.

Here is an entry from my journal, dated September 8, 1996:

> "Yesterday I went to see my father. As he has become more and more depressed, I've tried to be more and more cheerful. Most likely this act is a terrible drain for him. It is for me. But his silences are devastating. I burst out, 'Dad, you're hurting my feelings by not talking to me.' 'I don't feel like talking,' he said. 'Don't take it personally.'"

I took his silences as an accusation; I never understood that what he wanted was companionship, not entertainment. I didn't have to try so hard.

On Rosh Hashanah, the start of the new Jewish year, I'll visit your grave, with its granite headstone the color of fresh earth. I'll place a small rock on top to mark my visit. I'll utter a prayer for *refuah sh'lamah*, peace and healing in the world. We need that right now. Those are things you would have wanted, too.

It's time to lay my pen to rest.

To every thing there is a season, and a
time to every purpose under the
heaven;
a time to be born, and a time to die; a
time to plant, and a time to pluck up that
which is planted;
a time to kill, and a time to heal; a time
to break down, and a time to build up;
a time to mourn and a time to dance;
a time to cast away stones, and a time
to gather stones together; a time to
embrace, and a time to refrain from
embracing;
a time to get, and a time to lose; a time
to keep, and a time to cast away;
a time to rend, and a time to sew; a
time to keep silence, and a time to speak;
a time to love, and a time to hate; a
time of war, and a time of peace.

Ecclesiastes 3: 1–8

About the Author

Nancy Gerber holds a doctorate in Literatures in English from Rutgers University. She has taught in the English and Women's Studies departments at Rutgers University, Newark, New Jersey. The author of *Portrait of the Mother-Artist: Class and Creativity in Contemporary American Fiction* (Lexington Books, 2003), she lives in Montclair, New Jersey, with her family. She can be reached at n.gerber@worldnet.att.net.